Cape Town
A PLACE BETWEEN

HENRY TROTTER

Intimate Geographies Series

CATALYST PRESS

For further information, write Catalyst Press at info@catalystpress.org

In North America, this book is distributed by
Consortium Book Sales & Distribution, a division of Ingram.
Phone: 612/746-2600 | cbsdinfo@ingramcontent.com | www.cbsd.com

In South Africa, Namibia, and Botswana,
this book is distributed by LAPA Publishers.
Phone: 012/401-0700 | lapa@lapa.co.za | www.lapa.co.za

FIRST EDITION 10 9 8 7 6 5 4 3 2 1

Cover photo by © Henry Trotter, of Beatrix Court,
Manenberg, Cape Town, 2001
Cover design by Karen Vermeulen, Cape Town, South Africa

Library of Congress Cataloging-in-Publication Data

Names: Trotter, Henry, author.
Title: Cape Town : a place between / Henry Trotter.
Other titles: Intimate geographies series.
Description: First edition. | Livermore, CA : Catalyst Press, 2020.

Series: Intimate geographies series
Summary: "Cape Town is a place between.
Between two oceans, between first and third worlds,
between east and west..."
-- Provided by publisher.

Identifiers: LCCN 2019037022 (print) | LCCN 2019037023 (ebook)
ISBN 9781946395252 (paperback) | ISBN 9781946395283 (ebook)
Subjects: LCSH: Cape Town (South Africa)--Description and travel.
Cape Town (South Africa)--Social conditions.
Cape Town (South Africa)--Social life and customs.
Classification: LCC DT2405.C364 T76 2019 (print)
LCC DT2405.C364 (ebook) | DDC 968.7355--dc23
LC record available at https://lccn.loc.gov/2019037022
LC ebook record available at https://lccn.loc.gov/2019037023

ISBN 978-1946395252

Printed in Canada

Dedicated to Marjorie and Sonoya,

the two great loves of my life

TABLE OF CONTENTS

A PLACE BETWEEN

three fragments and an invitation

Let's start at the end. The end of the world. Day Zero.

After more than three years of drought, this was the day in 2018 that Cape Town was due to run dry. The dams would be puddles, the taps turned off, and residents would have to start queuing for daily water rations. With empty buckets and chapped lips, they'd be forced to muster at municipal water points, cursing their fate while drinking in the irony of it all.

They'd glimpse the vast oceans around them, thinking, "Water water everywhere, but not a drop to drink."

They'd remember the politicians who boasted this was the best run city in the country, wondering how they got into this mess.

And they'd give a hollow chuckle at the times they'd said—or heard others say—that Cape Town didn't have the same problems as the rest of Africa. It was "too developed."

Thankfully, the rains returned, the dam levels rose, and the city escaped this dreaded fate. And not a moment too soon. Cape Town was only a few months away from becoming the first large metropolis in the world to run out of water.

Capetonians did their best to stall this aquatic reckoning, letting "yellow mellow," placing bricks in their toilet cisterns, taking showers standing over buckets, using grey water to flush the toilets, and drilling bore holes to avoid using dam water.

The government also instituted water restrictions, fined water wasters, and invested in small desalination plants.

Of course, some folks claimed Day Zero was all a hoax, a scheme cooked up by the government to intimidate people into buying bottled water. If that was true (which it wasn't), then it certainly worked! To avoid drinking the brown, silty water sputtering from their faucets, people started buying way more bottled water.

This experience of "hydrological poverty" was a rude shock to the majority of Capetonians (80%) who enjoy indoor plumbing. Prior to that, they had taken for granted their ability to open up their taps and drink safe, clean water in their own homes. When this changed—coupled with the return of national electricity blackouts, or "loadshedding"—it seemed as if the city were on the brink of the apocalypse. (Coming soon, *Mad Max: Beyond Day Zero.*)

Meanwhile, the poorest Capetonians who live in shack dwellings wondered what the fuss was all about. They were used to queuing at communal taps for water and recycling what they could save. The rest of the metro could fret over its sudden exposure to water shortage, but for the poor, life carried on as usual.

For them, every day is Day Zero.

∿∿

A friend of the family, Astrid, lives in one of the townships on the outskirts of the city. She drives a lot for work, often returning home at late hours. One night as she was waiting alone at a traffic light at the top of a freeway offramp, a huge vehicle came speeding up and screeched to a halt just behind her. Two armed men jumped out and ran up to her windows, flanking her.

In panic, Astrid started flailing around, screaming, "Oh Lord, I'm dead! I'm dead! They're gonna kill me!"

As she cried out, the men yanked the front doors open. (The locks on her jalopy hadn't worked in years.) She looked at the man next to her and shrieked, "*Boetie* (brother), you're gonna kill me! I'm dead! You're gonna kill me!"

But the men put their hands up themselves and shook their heads, trying to calm her down, "*Sisi* (sister), sisi, no. We're not here to rob you. We need your help."

"Wait, what?" she thought.

"Sisi, *we're* about to get robbed!"

Astrid stopped yelling, confused. But the men immediately ran back to their vehicle—now clearly an armored cash-in-transit carrier in the rearview mirror—and started pulling out bags of money. They opened her back doors and began chucking bag after bag into the car. They didn't even bother to hide them. Just one after another onto the seats.

Astrid sat trembling. When the men were done, one looked her in the eye, "Sisi, we're about to get hit. We've been tipped off that we're the target of an inside job. Please keep this money safe for us. Our jobs are on the line. We'll see you in half an hour at the petrol garage in the township."

With that, they jumped in their van and sped off. They didn't exchange names, numbers or license info. They just left. This all went down in the space of about a minute.

Astrid sat alone at the lamp-lit intersection, her blinker still on for a right turn. The van was gone, red tail lights fading in the distance. But before she released her foot from the brake, she glanced at the bags behind her.

Considering how common cash-in-transit heists are in Cape Town, it seemed like the men must be telling the truth. Certainly *they* couldn't be the thieves, right? Or could they? But if they were about to get hit, then taking the money might put her in danger as well. And what if she got held up herself in her own dangerous township? This felt way out of control.

She then briefly imagined what she could do with the money. "My days of hoofing and hustling could be over! First class all the way!" But the thought of looking over her shoulder for the rest of her life seemed stressful, especially with a family to look after. Still, she mused, "I wonder how much is in there?"

She drove to the petrol garage and waited anxiously. A half-an-hour came and went. Then another hour. Cautiously, she went back to the offramp to trace the route the van had taken when it left her. A couple of miles later, she saw the van on the side of the road—now pocked by bullets—illuminated by the flashing lights of police cars and an ambulance.

As she pulled up, one of the guards stood next to the other who was lying on a stretcher. She could hear them talking to another man, "No *baas*, we didn't get her name. Or her number. But she was driving a purple car." Then they spotted her. "That car! There she is!" They almost cried with relief.

As it turned out, within minutes of leaving the money with Astrid, the guards were attacked by a gang of armed men. They exchanged gun fire and one of the guards took a bullet.

As she handed back the money, the guards whispered to her, "Sisi, you saved us. There were ten million Rands (US$700,000) in those bags!"

A pit instantly formed in her stomach. Somehow knowing the amount made it worse. She hugged the men, drove home and went straight to bed without saying a word.

A couple of weeks later, the boss of the firm gave Astrid ten thousand bucks (US$700) for her help. It wasn't quite the millions she could have had—"A millionaire for an hour," as she likes to say—but it came with fewer headaches.

File this one under: Only in Cape Town.

∿∿

Ahhhh, the festive season. School is out, the sun is shining, and the beaches beckon for summertime fun. These are the "Big Days" when Cape Town is at its best. The city swells with tourists while locals relax and enjoy the spoils of the city. There's a special vibe in the air.

So what could go wrong?

Recently, just before Christmas, locals were chilling at Clifton's magnificent Fourth Beach, watching the sun go down over the Atlantic. Nestled beneath the mountain and a posh collection of million dollar "bungalows," it's one of the most popular beaches in Cape Town.

But before the sun could descend beneath the waves, some private security guards started telling everyone to pack their bags and leave. Contracted by the (mostly white) residents of the bungalows, who had become worried about the growing prevalence of crime in the area, the guards said the beachgoers were breaking municipal by-laws, and therefore had to go. The sun-seekers objected, saying this was a public beach. Private security guards had no authority to enforce such laws. And no one was breaking them anyway. But within fifteen minutes, the crowds were cleared off the sand.

Most of them were black people.

Within days, this was all that Capetonians could talk about. Black beachgoers took to social media to complain about the racism they believed was motivating the guards to eject them. They said the guards' actions were just like the racist bad old days.

The security firm said that they were just helping the local police because two 15-year-olds had been recently raped there. They felt it was better to clear the beach rather than allow more crimes to take place. They pled innocence to the charge of racism.

The cops, though, said they had no record of any rape cases being investigated, making it appear that the security firm was lying. Only later did they admit being alerted to an incident where beachgoers stopped an apparent sexual assault against a 15-year-old girl. A spokesperson said, "the victim and her family refused to open a case against the suspect, who is known to them."

City officials, meanwhile, denied hiring the firm to help cops patrol the beach. They said it was not acting on their orders. They promised to investigate. So did Parliament.

The white ratepayers who had apparently employed the firm stayed mum, hoping the whole thing would blow over.

Enter the Black People's National Crisis Committee. A new lobbying group, formed in response to this very situation, the BPNCC called on "all self-respecting Blacks (Indian, coloured and Africans) [sic] to descend at Clifton 4th Beach...for a political protest." Proclaiming solidarity in a Facebook post with "our people" whose rights were violated at the beach, the group stated that the guards' actions smacked of apartheid, a time when blacks were not allowed to go to certain beaches. They said, "Enough talk, let's get there this Friday at 18h00 and cleanse the beach of racist spirits."

This cleansing process would involve slaughtering a sheep, calling on the ancestors to chase away the beach's "evil spirits," and renaming it after the anti-colonial Xhosa warrior, Makhanda. They said, "The offering of the sheep is calling on our ancestors to respond to our trauma at the hands of white people over the years."

This charge was made even more poignant when a local writer reminded Capetonians that this was the same beach where 200 slaves had drowned in the 1790s when a Portuguese slaver ran aground. Their bodies littered the shoreline while the survivors were sold off in town the very next day.

On the day of the protest, black people arrived in numbers. Word of the ceremony had spread on social media with the hashtag #ReclaimClifton.

Many white people were also there, some in support, some out of curiosity, but most in opposition. They were animal rights activists objecting to the slaughter of the "innocent" sheep.

The leader of the BPNCC, Chumani Maxwele, shout- ed to the crowd, "We are going to untie the sheep and walk it to the ocean to waken Nxele's (Makhanda's) spirit. Nxele's spirit is along this ocean. Down with white racists, down." He then cut the sheep's throat at the water's edge while protesters burnt incense. He declared, "Today, the dignity of the black people has been restored."

The animal rights folks were themselves incensed, yelling that "the only thing you know is to kill." Their verbal clashes with the protestors were recorded and uploaded on social media.

Despite the heated exchanges, the ceremony was peaceful by South African standards. And in the after- math, Capetonians tried to make sense of it all. (They still are, really.)

For the white ratepayers, this whole thing was blown way out of proportion. As residents of the area, they had hired private security to help make the place safer.

There was nothing strange about that. But that the firm cleared a public beach full of black people without any legal authority to do so? Well, that was an unfortunate misunderstanding.

For city officials, the incident was about jurisdiction and control. They frowned at the private firm's encroachment into public policing functions, promising to investigate. After the slaughter, they also threatened to charge the protest leaders for conducting the ritual in a public place without a permit.

For the animal rights activists, it boiled down to the sheep. They felt outraged that a defenseless animal had to lose its life so that humans could sort out a mess caused by other humans.

And for the black protestors, this was about how white racism remains alive and well in Cape Town. They argued that this wasn't an isolated incident, but part of a long history of humiliation and segregation. And the claim that the guards were responding because of a supposed rape was a smokescreen for their real intentions.

The aggrieved beachgoers could have responded to this situation in any number of ways (charging the firm, launching civil action against the ratepayers, or staging a beach sit-in), but the response that won the day was a cultural one. In a city used to protest through arson, vandalism and *toyi-toying* (protest dancing), this turn to ritual came as a shock to most. It was refreshing, disarming, and yet also strikingly provocative.

Cape Town has been historically hostile to public

expressions of African culture, unless packaged for mass consumption, so the call for black people to slaughter a sheep and invoke the ancestors—here, on *this* beach, in the heart of white opulence—was an electrifying prospect. That's how the BPNCC, a group of young rebels-at-the-ready who were not even in Clifton when the beachgoers were ejected, were able to direct how events unfolded thereafter.

On the one hand, this ceremonial strategy was pure theater. The drama of the ritual, and the fact that an animal was sacrificed on site, was inherently intriguing. And the entrance of the animal rights folks into the mix made it even *more* compelling. No one could look away.

On the other hand, such ceremonies were common for many South African communities, so it could not just be dismissed. It held moral force. For many African people, certainly, the ritual promised a sense of renewal at this highly fraught site.

The public response to this episode revealed the usual fault lines. Whites were called racists. Animals rights activists were told they shouldn't try to impose their values on other people. The private security firm was vilified for overreaching on behalf of its wealthy clients. The cops and politicians were dismissed as incompetent. Blacks were called oversensitive. The BPNCC were critiqued as opportunists who had hijacked the beach-goers' pain. And the legitimacy of the ceremony was even called into question since traditional leaders did not conduct it.

(Lost in the finger-pointing was the plight of the

teenage girl who was attacked by someone "known" to her family.)

The one thing most people could agree on, though, was that, through the ceremonial slaughter, Clifton was a different beach now. Whether people believed in the spiritual power of the ritual or not, the fact that it happened and that *some* people believed in it, meant that most Capetonians now had a different feeling about that beach. It may look the same, it may feel the same, and it may even *be* the same in every way that it was prior to the ceremony, but it was different. The ceremony—and the massive public debate it ignited— transformed it.

In people's minds.

∿∿

So, yah, Cape Town. Lots of fun.

If you're not busy googling "climate change refugee," then you're being coerced into helping security guards protect corporate South Africa's cash, or driving down the coastline looking for a good protest to join. There's always something to keep you on your toes.

These three stories give you a glimpse of the kind of memorable moments that can happen here, but are just fragments of a larger story about life in this remarkable city. A city where, as these stories hint, four million people straddle the line between abundance and scarcity, vulnerability and violence, insecurity and belonging. A city united by its peculiar divisions.

It's a place that defies easy understanding, as well,

no matter how long you've lived here. Just when you think you've got it licked, it knocks you around and demands a rethink. It's as exciting as it is exhausting.

That's because, as I want to show in the pages that follow: Cape Town is *a place between*.

Between two oceans. Between first and third worlds. Between east and west. Between past and future.

So too are most of its residents, the Cape coloureds. A group between black and white. Between native and settler. Between African and European. A people between.

Indeed, Cape Town is the only metropole on the sub-Saharan mainland where the majority of inhabitants are not black Africans. Their presence and the particular history of this city throws into doubt the standard dichotomies (black/white, African/Western, developed/ underdeveloped) that we rely on to make sense of this land and who inhabit it.

That is why you will often hear locals and visitors agree that Cape Town is not the *real* Africa. Africa is somewhere else. Upcountry. Out there. But not here.

So how can we make sense of this captivating city that is most assuredly *in* Africa, but not, seemingly, *of* it?

In this slim volume, I ask you to join me in exploring this curious corner of the continent. It's a quirky and challenging city, for sure, but full of surprising rewards. And as we ponder the peninsula's history, politics, culture, and prospects, let us do so with open minds, free of the preconceptions that often inhibit a greater understanding of Africa and those who live here. Let us embrace the discomfort, the dissonance, and the delight entailed in investigating this inimitable city called Cape Town.

A place between.

∿∿

Welcome my friends. *Wamkelekile. Welkom.* Glad you're here. Let me just note a few things before we continue.

First, this book offers an *intimate geography* of Cape Town, emerging from my personal relationship with the city over the last two decades. In it, I do my best to give an accurate and representative understanding of this place for you, but it remains idiosyncratic, partial, and incomplete. Exactly what you should expect from an exploration of a city as diverse as this.

Because of that, it's also something of an experiment. It's not a traditional guide book, though it would be a useful companion to one. Those books direct you to iconic destinations, while this one helps you understand the relationship between those icons and the worlds beyond, where Capetonians make meaning in their lives. It's not a memoir either, even if I do share a lot of my own memories. I offer them to help make sense of the city in an accessible way. And it's not a travelogue, as I'm not a visitor. I live here. Shall we call it a live-o-logue? (No. That sounds ridiculous.) In any case, it's a reflective look at the city I now call home, punctuated with anecdotes, arguments and, hopefully, insights.

Thankfully, my life in Cape Town has included some

wild and wonderful times with protesters, politicians, prostitutes, professors, pupils, minstrels, gangsters, sailors, forced removees, and many other folks across the peninsula. They all make an appearance here. I hope you'll find my interactions with them both enlightening and entertaining. After all, this isn't a dull city, and I won't speak of it as such.

Second, I realize there's nothing quite like listening to a white American guy man-splaining African history and culture. Even *I* cringe when I think about that. And, no doubt, this book reveals as much, if not more, about me as it does Cape Town. That is why I've embraced my limitations and offered a subjective, personal take on the city. My contribution here should be seen as but one of many.

If you are a local, I hope this volume allows you to see your city from a different perspective, adding to and complicating your own understanding of it. If you are a visitor, I hope it offers the knowledge necessary for unpacking the many types of situations you will encounter here. There's a lot of historical, cultural, and emotional complexity in everything you will see. I hope this book gives you access to some of this, making your experiences more meaningful.

Lastly, as we dive deeper, we have to make peace with the fact that race still matters in South Africa. We won't be able to get around that here. We must deal with it openly and honestly. This means that I will use the same racial terms that Capetonians use to make sense of their reality. Contested, unsettled words like:

- *Africans*—the indigenous Bantu-speaking
  majority of South Africa, of which the Xhosa
  are the primary African residents in Cape Town.
- *coloureds*—the genetically diverse majority
  of Cape Town whose ancestors include
  indigenous Khoisan herders, Indonesian slaves,
  Southern and West Africans, European sailors
  and settlers, and many more.
- *Indians*—people historically emanating from
  the sub-continent with a huge presence in
  Durban, and a smallish one in Cape Town.
- *blacks*—Africans, coloureds and Indians as a
  single political unit (a better term for referring
  to these groups together than "non-whites,"
  but which, in everyday parlance, is usually used
  to refer to Africans).
- *whites*—descendants largely of Anglo (British)
  and Dutch (Afrikaner) settlers, plus smaller
  numbers of Portuguese, Greeks, and Eastern
  European Jews.

Of course, one might have hoped that the New South Africa (the Rainbow Nation!) might have been able to move beyond such burdensome terminology, inaugurating a post-racial future, but that hasn't happened yet.

And while the emotional hues surrounding these terms have changed over time, they remain meaningful in the lives of Capetonians. And they are also complicated by other aspects of locals' identities, such as their gender, class, sexuality, language, religion, age, health status, and physical ability.

So, I use the locally relevant racial and cultural terms here for practical purposes, not because I endorse them. Indeed, one wades into the treacherous waters of Cape Town race relations at one's own peril. Let's do it together, shall we?

CITYSCAPE

a lyrical portrait

Understanding Cape Town starts with the senses.

It begins as you *feel* the relentless push and pull of the southeaster, shoving you forwards, backwards, sideways.

As you *hear* the crashing of the waves from one end of the peninsula to the other, keeping time with the *gqom* beats of throbbing minibus taxis.

As you *taste* the savory *boerewors*, piquant biryani, hearty *bredie*, briny snoek, and syrupy *koeksisters*, washed down with rooibos tea, Bashews cola, Castle lager, Winelands Pinotage.

As you *smell* the aromatic curry wafting across the Cape Flats mixed with a dash of acrid smoke from field burns and brush fires.

And, more than anything, as you *see*. As you take in with your eyes one of the most beautiful and dramatic urban landscapes in the world. Dominated from every direction by the imposing grandeur of Table Mountain, whose majesty makes supplicants of all who stand before it (see image 1).

Indeed, it is Nature that defines the contours of an initial understanding of this city. It is a fact so overwhelming that, for many, it is the only feature that will be experienced or remembered from a visit here. Of course, it is so much more than that, but for both locals and visitors, the sheer audacity of the Cape's natural bounty can subsume all else, can comprehensively capture one's consciousness.

But while the visual tends to dominate any interaction with this environment—at least initially—it is in the physical engagement with it through walking, hiking, meandering, touching, smelling, playing, swimming, that a more equitable relationship emerges. Between nature and the self. When the Mountain is no longer up there, but under one's feet. When Kirstenbosch's exotic florals no longer form a scenic tableau, but sit under one's nose. And when the ocean's cold, blue power not only shapes the gentle curve of the coast, but buoys one's body from a wave's crest to a foamy cradle.

This is what makes Cape Town so special for so many. It is the promise that you can step outside from almost anywhere, turn your neck and face the Mountain. Or that, on a whim, you can venture to any number of beaches with a snack in hand to catch the last rays of the sun before it dips beneath the horizon. It is an outrageous privilege.

And its offerings are endless: Table Mountain, Lion's Head, Signal Hill, Table Bay, Robben Island, Hout Bay, Chapman's Peak, Noordhoek, Cape Point, False Bay, Constantia, the Winelands, and more. One never feels fully worthy of the easy access we have to such beauty.

But talk to locals and they'll reveal an ambivalence about these natural wonders. For how should we feel about Table Mountain knowing that it is where runaway slaves used to hide themselves from pursuing slave-owners and soldiers? Where, today, its trails remain a hunting ground for thieves who have preyed on hikers for years. The slopes of this hill are covered in violence.

How can we enjoy the roses of Kirstenbosch's botanical gardens when the barb of apartheid's legacy pricks the conscience, knowing that the families who used to live and work there were forcibly removed from their homes to the sandy wastelands of the Cape Flats? This soil has been sown with tears.

And how can we delight in the sophisticated vibe and inviting waters of Camps Bay when, for much of its recent history, people of the "wrong color" were denied access to this beach, ejected with the nudge of a baton? This coastline is littered with memories of injustice and humiliation.

Nevertheless, most still find a way to enjoy the Cape's largesse, if they have the means. Residents still go up the mountain, smell the flowers, and frolic in the waves. But the relationship between locals and this landscape is complicated. There is a love for it, yes—a proud, aching attachment, even—but it is combined with a quiet indignation that this beauty has been stripped of its innocence. Tarnished by the human history that has so enveloped it.

Cape Town is a slice of Eden buried in half-eaten apples.

So while an understanding of Cape Town may start with an appreciation of its natural virtues, greater insight can only come with the more delicate process of grappling with its history, culture, and politics. It is then that we can confront its glitzy and gritty urban landscape that has not only been the backdrop to a history of genocide, slavery, and apartheid, but of resistance, rebellion, and liberation. A site where stories of empowerment and upliftment are told alongside those of poverty and desperation.

This is a city of "both and" / "neither nor."

A sun-drenched peninsula best glimpsed through a prism noir.

∿

All of this is to say that the burden of history can weigh heavily here. That is, if you can ever get over your paralyzing fear of the present. Indeed, Cape Town is one of the deadliest cities in the world, right up there with Caracas and Tijuana. The murder rate in some of the townships defies belief, resembling that of warzones. Domestic abuse is prevalent, revealing deep tensions in some communities about the status of women in an age of increasing gender rights. And the opening salvo for any form of communication between the people and the government is not a strongly worded letter to the editor, but an act of arson, the start of a riot, or the hurling of shit at public buildings.

While this picture is highly fragmented, with the poor bearing the brunt of this violence far more than the well-to-do who can afford high walls, razor wire, burglar bars, and private security, no one who lives in Cape Town has been untouched by some shocking or banal act of personal violation. Almost everyone has a horror story.

In my family alone, my sister-in-law was tied up and held at gunpoint while criminals robbed her house. My brother-in-law was shot in the stomach while sitting in his car in front of his house. Another brother-in-law lost all of his worldly possessions to a gang of thieves who had been targeting his neighborhood. My wife had her purse snatched off her shoulder while riding the train. And I had my cellphone grabbed out of my hand while walking down the street.

But this is nothing. We've been quite fortunate. We personally know—as does every Capetonian— people who have been raped, murdered, stabbed, or kidnapped. Parents who have lost children to stray bullets shot from a teenage gangster's gun. Mothers who have had their newborns snatched from their arms while sleeping at the maternity ward.

And many of us know perpetrators of these terrible acts. Indeed, we often know them as our kin and loved ones.

The normalcy of all of this means that we live in a constant state of vigilance and…well…fear.

And this fact, this simmering anxiety, damages us. The entire society. No one is immune.

It is hard to feel truly free, fully open, or even mini-mally trusting in this environment. Everyone's skittish. Paranoid. On edge.

∿

But my word.

Despite all this. Despite the crime, despite the un-employment, despite the stagnant economy, despite the droughts, despite it all—I can't help but feel invigorated and grateful to live in this beautiful mess.

What a city!

Edge of the continent. Cauldron of cultures.

Where Afrikaans—an Asian-infused European language born and bred in Africa—was first written down by literate Imams in the Arabic script.

Where the descendants of slaves adopted the comic-ironic style and swagger of itinerant black American music troupes to annually celebrate—nay, to claim—their belonging to this city. Expressed through that most memorable and baffling of characters: the Coon.

And where the culinary traditions of meat and mielie grilling Africans mix

with sausage and rusk savoring Afrikaners
with soup and tea sipping Anglos
with duck and noodle dishing Chinese
with *gatsby* and *potjie* grazing coloureds
with dahl and roti devouring Indians
with lox and latke loving Jews
with curry and samosa cooking Malays
with fish and chicken feasting Portuguese
with—well—just about every other cuisine on
the planet.

I mean, c'mon, this is where Dollar Brand, Robbie Jansen, Basil Coetzee, Errol Dyers and Winston Mankuku Ngozi pioneered the unmistakable melodies of Cape Jazz.

Where Brenda Fassie, the Queen of African Pop, was born.

Where Christiaan Barnard performed the world's first successful heart transplant.

And where Nelson Mandela cast his eyes for two decades from his prison abode on Robben Island—so close, yet so far.

This is a city where cultures collide, co-mingle, connect. Where a heady mix of collective ethnic traditions and eccentric individual experimentations lead to surprising new forms of expression and possibility.

A city big enough to be a vanguard of cultural creativity across the continent, but small enough for anyone with grit, focus, and fearlessness to make a name for themselves.

There's just something about it.

A city that draws you in. Forcefully at first, with visual magnetism. But more subtly, later, as its cultural vitality works on you. Changes you. Ruins you for all other places.

BETWEEN TWO OCEANS

history, memory, amnesia

I first came to Africa in 1994 when South Africa teetered on a knife's edge. In the months leading up to its first democratic elections that year, the country seethed with violence.

In KwaZulu-Natal, African National Congress (ANC) and Inkatha Freedom Party (IFP) loyalists were engaged in a vicious regional war, fomented by a shadowy "third force" within the apartheid security apparatus.

East of Johannesburg, the charismatic South African Communist Party (SACP) leader Chris Hani was assassinated at his home by two white men. Nelson Mandela himself had to beg the nation not to tear itself apart over this outrage.

And in Cape Town, the white American Fulbright student Amy Biehl was stabbed and stoned by young activists in Gugulethu township. They had just attended a rally where the cry of "one settler, one bullet" (kill the whites) still rang in their ears when they came across Biehl who was dropping off university colleagues.

As a 20-year-old student myself then, going into my third year of university in California and dreaming about where I could study abroad, South Africa was not an option. Not by a longshot. It was still run by the National Party, the white supremacists who initiated apartheid and were scrambling to protect their privileges. And they were opposed by one of the most politically mobilized populations on earth, an "ungovernable" people who had been engaged in an endless series of protests, boycotts, stay-aways, strikes, and sabotage campaigns since the Soweto uprising of 1976.

I had to admit, from what I knew about the country then—through newspaper headlines mostly—I found South Africa to be thoroughly intimidating. Completely hard core. And its people seemed just a *weeee* bit intense.

So at the time, Zimbabwe was the place to go in Africa. Safe, stable, peaceful, with an excellent education system, Zim was a popular destination for college exchange programs. Renowned as "the breadbasket of Southern Africa," the country seemed poised for a bright future.

Seeking to expand my cultural horizons, I signed up to study African literature and the Shona language at the University of Zimbabwe (UZ) in Harare. I even wrote a letter to then-President Mugabe before I arrived, letting him know that I was excited to visit his country. (He never wrote back.)

During my year at UZ, I learned as much as I could about African history, culture, politics, and literature. I read widely and took advantage of the easy access that Zimbabweans offered of their time and thoughts. And I also took trips to the rural areas and neighboring countries, including South Africa after the surprisingly peaceful elections. Went twice to Durban, a beach bum's paradise at the time.

But after UZ, I didn't want my time in Africa to end, so I got a job teaching English literature at a ritzy private boys' high school next to the President's house in Harare. Steeped in Anglo-Rhodesian traditions, the racially diverse students wore white collared shirts, red ties, khaki shorts, knee-high socks, blazers, and floppy cricket hats. They would stand and doff their caps, saying "Sir," whenever I passed by. Sadly, such courtesy did not extend to the country's immigration officers who denied my application for a visa extension after six months of teaching. Apparently, I didn't have any "essential skills" that Zimbabwe couldn't live without. (I still don't.)

So, I strapped on my backpack and started wandering around East Africa, plodding through Malawi, Zambia, and Tanzania, then up to Uganda, Rwanda, and Burundi, then east to Kenya, and north to Ethiopia and Eritrea. Then I flew over to Madagascar and Mauritius for some months, then back to Southern Africa again to explore Mozambique, South Africa, Namibia, and Botswana, eventually ending my sojourn in Cameroon.

Four years. Seventeen countries. It was awesome!

But as I traveled, I embarked on a personal mission. Everywhere I went, I searched out bookshops and bought as many local titles as I could find. Then I'd read them while in the country, inviting the literary renderings of these artists to enhance my own experiences. This massively expanded my mental and emotional engagement with these places.

It was in this way that I first got a glimpse of Cape Town, through a book I found while recovering from bilharzia in Lilongwe, the capital of Malawi. (Bilharzia is a liver fluke I got from swimming in Lake Malawi. Not pleasant. Don't google it.)

I took the strangely titled novel, *Buckingham Palace: District Six*, back to my fleabag hotel-cum-brothel next to the bus station and devoured it. Even with all the noises permeating the flimsy room partitions, I began to glimpse a curious world that I had yet to encounter in my travels on the continent. One that challenged my notions of the complexity, diversity and cultural parameters of "Africa."

It was a creole world. A mixed world. An in-between world. It stood between the conceptions that I had always taken for granted about Africa and Europe, black and white, east and west. An unsettling and intriguing world. One that I would definitely have to see for myself.

Written by Richard Rive, *Buckingham Palace* tells the story of the residents of a block of flats in District Six, the historical heart of Cape Town's "mixed race" coloured population. Written after the district was destroyed by apartheid bulldozers, the book recounts the sights, sounds, personalities, and wit of the area. It revels in the vitality of the street life, the inventiveness of the mixed Afrikaans and English speech (*Kaapse taal*), and the quality of the relationships between the people there of all racial backgrounds. Here was a story about a place similar to Harlem for African-Americans in its cultural and historical import for a group of people that I knew almost nothing about: Cape coloureds. A people, I'd soon learn, whose presence in this corner of the continent challenged any simplistic answers to the question of, "Who is an African?"

∿

For hundreds of years, the area around the Cape Peninsula was a seasonal pastureland for indigenous Khoi herders who moved around the region, hunting and foraging. This differentiated them from their more settled Bantu-speaking neighbors to the east, like the Xhosa, who plowed fields of millet and grazed longhorn cattle. Various Khoi would have interacted with these peoples—leading the Xhosa to incorporate the Khoi's click sounds into their language—but the Khoi were largely on their own in this corner of the continent.

Their relative isolation was due to a simple fact of meteorology: in the southwest part of this region, rain falls in the winter; everywhere else, the summer. This is why Bantu agro-pastoralists like the Xhosa, who raised crops and cattle on grasses reliant upon summer rainfall, were settled eastward of this area.

By the 1500s, the Portuguese had rounded the Cape of Good Hope, but never established a foothold here. That may have been due to the fact that, in 1510, the Khoi killed Portuguese big-shot Francisco de Almeida (the Iberians' first viceroy of India) and dozens of his soldiers in retaliation for the theft of their cattle after coming ashore. So for the next 150 years, thousands of wind-tossed European sailors anchored in Table Bay, trading with the Khoi for meat while writing tall tales about them for fascinated audiences back home. But they never settled.

Eventually, as the battle between European powers for control over the lucrative spice trade intensified, the directors of the Dutch East India Company saw the Cape as perfectly located between their head-quarters in Amsterdam and the fragrant riches of the Spice Islands in the East Indies. A place that could act as a refreshment station for passing fleets. Though European forts already dotted the coasts of West and East Africa, servicing the Slave and Spice Trades, none of these led to white settlements because malaria and other tropical challenges kept them literally at bay. Fortunately for Europeans, there was no malaria at the Cape to wipe them out.

In 1652, the Company installed Jan van Riebeeck as the first colonial governor of the Cape. He oversaw the construction of a fort near the beach. Over time it was added to and remains today in the form of The Castle on the Foreshore.

To help him in his dealings with the Khoi, he hired a teenage girl, Krotoa—the niece of a local chieftain —to act as a go-between. Krotoa lived with the van Riebeecks, learned Dutch and Portuguese, and became an integral part of negotiations between her people and the foreigners she lived with. Between two worlds, Krotoa was a woman who stood at the center of in-digenous-colonial relations, like Pocahontas between the Native Americans and English in Virginia, and La

Malinche between the Aztecs and Spaniards in Mexico.

As the Khoi were loath to sell their cattle to the Company or give up their pasturage, relations between them were often tense. They faced off in battle on many occasions. But over time, the Dutch were able to project their power beyond the Fort, encouraging the migration of yet more settlers to the Cape. They established homesteads and farms, first near the Company settlement, then in the surrounding mountains at Stellenbosch and Paarl. Some French Huguenots fleeing Catholic persecution even ended up here, settling in Franschhoek and bringing with them their winemaking skills, helping give Cape Town a reputation as the Tavern of the Seas.

The expansion of European settlers did not bode well for the Khoi, nor for the San hunter-gatherers further afield. Their experiences resembled those of other indigenous peoples who encounter a more technologically complex society backed with their proverbial guns, germs, and steel. To chase the Khoisan off the land they desired, or to retaliate for Khoisan raids and incursions, the settlers organized into commandos to hunt down and exterminate Khoisan men, then enslave the women and children.

These settlers, and the multitudes of sailors passing through, brought with them diseases against which the Khoi were biologically defenseless. In waves, but especially in 1713, smallpox wiped out countless numbers of them.

∿

During this period, slaves were imported from Dutch and other European outposts in Indonesia, India, Mauritius, Madagascar, Mozambique, and West Africa. Dutch authorities enslaved rebellious types across the East Indies, relocating them to the Cape as a means of securing control of the Spice Islands. Some of them were Muslim clerics who brought with them their mystical Sufi Islamic belief system, an introduction dating to the city's founding in the 1650s.

The slave system spread far beyond Cape Town, going hand-in-hand with settler expansion. With it came the gradual conquest and assimilation of the Khoisan peoples into the colonial economy. Once free to roam the land with their cattle, enjoying the diverse vegetation they could gather along the way, they were stripped of their bovine wealth and compelled to work as agrarian laborers on European farms.

Over time, the Khoi's culture was lost, their heritage obliterated, their language unspoken and forgotten—at least for their descendants in Cape Town.

At the turn of the 18th Century, the Dutch lost the Cape to the British. Napoleon had made the Netherlands a vassal state, so the Brits secured this distant colony as a means of preventing French claims. Thereafter a gradual stream of British settlers arrived, expanding the boundaries of the colony eastward and introducing greater Anglo linguistic, legal, and cultural influence.

The casual dominance that the English felt at this time—boasting an empire upon which the sun never set—meant that their subjects were not only useful for labor, but entertainment as well. The citizens back home in England longed for a glimpse of the exotic flora, fauna, and people they possessed abroad, so in 1810, a Khoi woman name Sarah Baartman was sent to Britain and exhibited as the "Hottentot Venus" at a number of freak shows. Her comparatively short stature and supposedly amplified physical attributes made her a curiosity in the eyes of Europeans. She was later sold to an animal trainer in France, where she was paraded publicly, then later examined, measured, studied, and—after her death at age 26—dissected and displayed in the name of "science."

∿

In the 1830s, the British outlawed slavery across its possessions, including the Cape. This did not sit well with many Dutch families in the region whose livelihoods were based on a slave economy. They decided to load up their ox wagons and trek into the interior beyond the reach of British law, with their slaves and bonded Khoi in tow. This move away from coastal proximity marks the moment one can say that these "Dutch" settlers became "Afrikaners." Their descendants later memorialized this migration as the Great Trek.

But in Cape Town itself, emancipation marked a real—if limited—change in the legal and political circumstances for the ex-bonded. As the Cape gained greater autonomy over its internal affairs from London, a "liberal" civil order allowed property-owning men of all racial backgrounds to participate in electoral proceedings, at least in theory. Though this property qualification meant that few men of color—and no women at all—would have been able to vote, it created an opening for some upwardly mobile ex-bonded to leverage.

When diamonds were found in Kimberley in 1869 and gold in the Witwatersrand in 1886, a gold rush ensued with prospectors, pimps, and prostitutes flooding into southern Africa from around the world (including old hands from the California gold rush of 1849). Transiting through ports like Cape Town, many characters ended up staying in the city. But the economic boom this ignited led to massive infrastructural investment in the Cape, encouraging African laborers to seek work here.

Prior to this, there hadn't been many Bantu-speaking Africans in Cape Town. And there hadn't been much need to make clear distinctions between them and the others who descended from slaves, indigenous Khoisan, or mixed European backgrounds. Some of these differences would have been already meaningful socially, but they had not been politically or legally defined. The arrival of large numbers of Africans suddenly made this an issue.

In a context where white supremacy was taken for granted, new questions emerged:

- Should local "brown" subordinates belong to the same legal grouping as "tribal"

Africans, since all were "non-white"? Or should they be distinguished from each other in recognition of their differing historical, cultural, and linguistic backgrounds?

- Should those of predominantly Khoisan ancestry be distinguished from those of mainly slave origin? Or should they comprise a single group since they were both assimilated to the colonial culture through a shared history of exploitation?

- And what of those who appear mostly white, but have some other ancestry as well?

These were open questions between the late 1880s and the early 1900s. Educated elites from the assimilated subaltern community argued that—for racial, cultural, and linguistic reasons—they should be seen as distinct from Africans and treated accordingly. The most prominent proponent of this view was Dr. Abdullah Abdurahman, a Muslim medical doctor who entered Cape Town municipal politics at the turn of the century and pushed the cause of his emerging community.

Legislators agreed and codified this into law, creating hard identity boundaries where softer ones had previously prevailed. And while there were many twists in this tale of ethnogenesis, ultimately the culturally and genetically diverse "Cape people" began to be recognized—and to see themselves—as "coloureds."

Not black, not white, but in-between.

∿

After the merciless South African War of 1899–1902 (the "Boer War"), which pitted upcountry Afrikaners against the British Empire, the whites reconciled politically and integrated their territories. Britain's Cape Colony and Natal were united with the Afrikaners' Orange Free State and Transvaal to form the Union of South Africa in 1910. While Afrikaners typically led the national governments from the capital Pretoria, they were under the heavy influence of English mining and manufacturing interests. This was a practical, yet uncomfortable, compromise for Afrikaners who otherwise burned with rage at the atrocities committed against them by the Brits. Indeed, it is from that war that we get the term "concentration camp," when thousands of imprisoned Afrikaner women and children died from starvation and disease.

This uneasy relationship between rival white tribes defined national politics for the next decades. And as increasingly repressive legislation emanated from Pretoria, distant Cape Town came to be seen—especially by the English who held sway here—as a space of racial tolerance in contrast to the less subtle forms of racial domination favored by Afrikaners elsewhere. Comfortably nestled in their southern suburb cottages and estates, Cape Town's English whites could enjoy their tea and biscuits while their African nannies raised their children, their coloured chars cleaned their homes, and their "garden boys" tended to their prized poinsettias, telling themselves that the hired help were "just like family."

∿

Anglos' self-satisfied sense of unquestioned superiority came to a swift and shocking end when the National Party won the 1948 elections. English hegemony was broken by an ascendant Afrikaner *volk*. This meant that, at least in the Cape, their carefully calibrated paternalistic racism had to give way to a more piti- less—and crude—form of oppression. The pretense of the Brits' "civilizing mission" was supplanted by the Afrikaner state's grim determination to separate the races—deemed "natural enemies"—from each other.

In Cape Town, the apartheid era (1948–1994) was determined by a series of racial restrictions, most in- troduced in the 1950s by the national government, including the:

- *Population Registration Act:* defining South Africans racially as African, European, Indian or (if not one of these three, then) coloured.
- *Prohibition of Mixed Marriages Act:* exactly what it says.
- *Immorality Act:* criminalizing inter-racial sex.
- *Group Areas Act:* carving up urban areas into racial zones, forcing everyone to live in their designated areas.
- *Pass Laws Act:* requiring Africans over the age of 16 to carry "pass books" while in "white areas."

    Separate Amenities Act: differentiating public
    amenities like schools, buses, train carriages,
    boaches, building entrances, drinking
    fountains, and toilets according to race, with
    whites enjoying access to the best ones.

One dehumanizing law after another. And made all
the more ironic by the fact that the rest of the world
was finally starting to move away from such extreme
forms of racism. But the government was undeterred.
In 1961, as Britain's African colonies began shrugging
off imperial rule for independence, South Africa with-
drew from the Commonwealth and became a Republic,
cutting the Cape's long ties to Britain. The "winds of
change" that were sweeping across the continent were
met with stiff resistance in Africa's first—and last—
white colony.

As the legal policies of apartheid started to bite,
Africans across the country protested in increasingly
large numbers. In 1960, at a rally in Sharpeville initiated
by Robert Sobukwe of the Pan Africanist Congress
(PAC), thousands of Africans burned their hated pass
books, daring the authorities to arrest them all. The
police did just that, right after opening fire on them,
killing 69 people and wounding hundreds more.

A week after the massacre, Philip Kgosana of the
PAC led a march of more than 30,000 Africans from
Langa township to the Caledon Square police head-
quarters in Cape Town. They called for the state to
arrest them for not carrying their passes. Kgosana was
arrested, a nationwide state of emergency was

declared, and the PAC and the ANC were banned, leading to a massive manhunt for their leadership.

For the next 15 years, the state consolidated its power, hounding its political opponents through a powerful security apparatus. But in June 1976, as thousands of school students—inspired by the Black Consciousness Movement's focus on psychological emancipation—peacefully protested in Soweto against having to complete certain subjects in Afrikaans, the state's response marked the beginning of its end. Over the course of two teargas-filled days, the state gunned down hundreds of African children and youth, injuring thousands more. News of the uprising and brutal crackdown shocked the world, leading to international sanctions and isolation.

For the next decade, South Africa—and Cape Town in particular—became a site of ceaseless overt and covert political action, usually met with unremitting state violence.

Many older Capetonians still remember not only the chaos of the 1976 State of Emergency, but those of 1980, 1985, and 1986 as well. Years when fear, thus anger and determination reigned. When the writing of a poem could land you in jail, detained without trial. When armored personnel carriers patrolled the townships, soldiers with automatic rifles at the ready. When German shepherds strained at the leash, their handlers' wooden batons and coiled *sjamboks* (whips) swinging from utility belts.

But there came a point at which even the staunchest

defenders of apartheid could see that it would devour them as well. The wrath of those that had been so long oppressed would surely overwhelm them, as they had in the settler regimes in Angola, Mozambique, and Zimbabwe.

It turned out that, because Cape Town was home to Robben Island—a beautiful isle in Table Bay which, like Alcatraz, no one had ever thought of using for any other purpose than banishment, quarantine, and incarceration—the city hosted secret meetings between Nelson Mandela and the regime which was trying to back its way out of apartheid while preserving the gains whites had made under it.

When Mandela was released in 1990 after 27 years in prison, he gave his first speech on the balcony of Cape Town's City Hall to a jubilant crowd of 50,000 on the Grand Parade. An epic moment.

And just four years later, after the country's first democratic elections, Mandela reflected during his inauguration speech that, "Perhaps it was history that ordained that it be here, at the Cape of Good Hope, that we should lay the foundation stone of our new nation. For it was here at this Cape, over three centuries ago, that there began the fateful convergence of the peoples of Africa, Europe, and Asia on these shores."

Fateful indeed.

∿

So: Genocide? Check.

Slavery? Check.

Land expropriation? Check.

Forced relocations? Check.

Segregation? Check.

Labor exploitation? Check.

Cultural obliteration? Check.

Religious annihilation? Check.

Patriarchal domination? Check.

A legacy of intractable inequality? Check.

A checklist of human misery, to be sure, yet common to the histories of so many other white settler colonies like Australia, Canada, Namibia, Tasmania, and the United States. Indeed, the parallels to the history of my own country are striking.

As a historian, so much of my mental time is spent thinking about this hard, brutal history that has shaped this city. But as someone who lives here now, I know how a bird's eye view of the past, focused on the major events and themes, can miss a lot of essential details. After all, there is so much more to Cape Town's story than this seeming litany of unremitting woe. Even during colonialism and apartheid, Africans, coloureds, and Indians understood their lives as more than just oppression and struggle.

For every memory of a frightful interaction with the state, they remember dozens more of treasured times with family, friends, and lovers. They look back and remember enjoying watching the latest Westerns at the *bioscope* (cinema), kicking homemade footballs on the streets with their mates, stealing kisses in the shadows of the township floodlights, savoring grandma's *bobotie* straight out of the oven, dancing to the latest *Hotstix* groove with cousins at a backyard party, welcoming new life at the maternity ward. Despite apartheid, Capetonians managed to create lives that were meaningful and, at some level, fulfilling.

And many black folks also insist that they enjoyed warm, genuine, and treasured relationships with some whites. Though there was no getting around the structural effects of the law, some say they were able to enjoy interactions beyond the *baas*/boy and madam/*meisie* complex. This wasn't the norm, but it was real for those who experienced such mutuality and recognition.

Since that time, much has happened to complicate residents' feelings about the past. But if you want to understand this Cape of Good Hope, this Mother City—terms that must seem almost ironic by now—you have to be aware of the jagged contours of this difficult history. You must grapple with the reality of black pain here. And you must acknowledge white culpability for much of that pain. In so doing, you will be able to see how the past continues to shape reality here in the present.

And, perhaps more importantly, you'll be able to see how Capetonians are striving so desperately to move beyond it. To liberate themselves from their past so that it is they who own their history, and not their history which owns them.

BETWEEN FIRST AND THIRD WORLDS
politics, inequality, vice

After 46 years of apartheid, and centuries of colonial rule, South Africa held its first fully democratic elections. On 27 April 1994, the chance for a new beginning.

The government declared a public holiday so the nation could vote. Stretched out in long, winding queues, the throngs of newly enfranchised waited patiently to cast their ballots. It was a beautiful experience. A memorable day that South Africans proudly recollect.

Nationally, the ANC won more than 60% of the vote, giving them control of Pretoria, most provincial governments, and Parliament.

But in the Western Cape, something peculiar happened.

Africans in the province voted overwhelmingly for the party of liberation, the ANC, led by Nelson Mandela. As expected.

Whites voted predominantly for the sponsors of apartheid, the National Party, led by FW de Klerk. A few also voted for the Democratic Party, a small group of Anglos notable for their finger-wagging speeches in Parliament. Again, as expected.

But, defying all expectations, coloureds ended up voting in massive numbers for the National Party, delivering provincial power back to the very knuckleheads who had stripped them of their voting rights during apartheid. The same jerks who had forcibly removed 150,000 of them from their homes in the Cape Peninsula under the Group Areas Act. The same twits who had treated them as second-class citizens during their entire lives.

As one coloured political analyst later mused in bewilderment: "Never before did an oppressed and exploited people vote for their oppressors and exploiters in their first-ever democratic election, meant to celebrate their liberation from them. Never. It is unheard of in the global history of colonialism and imperialism."

So, what on earth happened?!

∿∿

For a couple of years I had the privilege—or misfortune—of working for one of the political parties in South Africa's Parliament. Located downtown next to the Company Gardens, "Parly" is where South Africa's morally compromised like to assemble and call each other Honourable This and Honourable That. (Of course, I fit right in.)

I sent my resume to the ANC, PAC, Democratic Alliance (DA), Independent Democrats (ID), and Congress of the People (COPE), hoping to land a job which would allow me to learn about South African politics from within the belly of the beast.

I took a researcher post with the first—well, the only—party to get back in touch with me. (I won't say which. I'm taking that to my grave.) I spent my days conducting research on educational and political matters for party MPs, writing press statements, and

developing policy positions. I also looked into the she-
nanigans of rival parties' politicians, sometimes calling
on the Public Protector or South African Human Rights
Commission to investigate them for maladministration,
corruption, fraud, and so forth. A few of these cases
led to headline-grabbing revelations that embarrassed
some of the less crafty politicos, making them feel
slightly uncomfortable for, well, about two minutes.
(You're welcome, South Africa!)

It was a thrill to join in the cut and thrust of political
skullduggery. But it was less inspiring to realize parliament's disinterest in acting as an executive watchdog.
The body was more of a rubber stamp to the President's
desires than a check on Ministerial power. Still, it was
a great place for me to gain a better understanding of
national and local politics.

Unlike the American political context I come from,
where two parties argue about the same things year
after year, the South African scene is refreshingly
diverse. There are more than a dozen legitimate parties,
based around ideology, religious convictions, workers'
rights, revolutionary idealism, single-issue reforms,
personality cults, or straight-up nut-bag nonsense.
Together they create a rich cacophony of (often tone-
deaf) voices.

At the top of the heap is the ANC, the party that has
dominated national politics since the end of apartheid.
It is a "broad church" balancing the demands of trade
unionists, communists, liberals, nationalists, and tra-
ditionalists. It is responsible for the impressive strides

taken to ensure greater access to housing, healthcare, and education for the poor across the country, just as it is also responsible for the rise in political corruption over the past years.

Nipping at its heels is the official opposition party, the DA. The result of an alliance between the New National Party and the Democratic Party in 2000, it espouses classical liberalism, promoting individual rights, meritocracy, and equal opportunity. It has built its reputation on "good governance" and holding the ANC to account, but is often critiqued as being a "party for minorities."

In addition to these heavyweights, some of the other notable parties (which I'm going to have some fun describing) include:

- *Economic Freedom Fighters (EFF)*: former ANC Youth League rabble-rousers who turned Parliament into a laugh-a-minute circus
- *Inkatha Freedom Party (IFP):* the organizational embodiment of Mangosotho Buthelezi's ego, the patriarch of Zulu nationalism
- *Freedom Front Plus (FF+):* family-run whites-only party promoting Afrikaner nationalism
- *African Christian Democratic Party* (ACDP): self-righteous blow-hards obsessed with prostitution and abortion
- *Congress of the People (COPE):* loyalists of former President Thabo Mbeki who, after Mbeki's demise, left the ANC, then back-

stabbed each other into a collective political coma

At the provincial and municipal level, there are also some smaller, niche parties that have vied for Capetonians' votes. Some of these will make you want to laugh or cry, or both:

- *Cape Party:* delusional provincial secessionists
- *Kingdom Governance Movement*: anti-gay millenarians trying to delay the anti-Christ's rise to worldwide domination
- *Al Jama-ah:* filling the "Shari'ah values" gap in the political marketplace
- *Dagga Party:* marijuana lovers so high, they keep forgetting to register themselves in time for getting on the ballot
- *Ubuntu Party:* started by a white guy who wants to abolish the South African Reserve Bank (oh boy, here we go), dabbling in Holocaust denial as well for good measure (uuuuv course)

So, you'll agree, it's all good, clean fun here. Something for everyone.

Even with all of these parties, the ANC has won every national election since 1994 as well as most provincial and municipal elections across the country, prompting former president Jacob Zuma to say that the party would rule until Jesus Christ returns. (Which might be sooner than he thinks.)

The DA, meanwhile, has consolidated much of the minority vote across the country and has won the

Western Cape province and the City of Cape Town over the past couple of election cycles. It also managed to take the metros of Port Elizabeth, Pretoria, and Johannesburg from the ANC through coalitions.

Since then, the DA has struggled to maintain internal cohesion while the ANC has been reeling from the results of the many investigation into "state capture" showing just how corrupt the organization became during the Zuma era. All of this means that, as ever, the political landscape in this city remains wide open.

∿

Back to '94, when the coloureds voted in the party of apartheid. A real head-scratcher that, and over the years, there have been no end of explanations proffered for this result. Some said that coloureds voted for "the devil that they knew rather than the devil they didn't." (Just being cautious.)

Others said that coloureds felt betrayed by the ANC for co-opting and disbanding the United Democratic Front (UDF), the mass anti-apartheid movement that many coloureds participated in during the 1980s. (A-ha, payback time!)

Some also suggested that coloureds were mental hostages to white racism, victims of a collective Stockholm Syndrome. (The old mass psychosis argument.)

Many were blunter in their estimation: coloureds are racist, pure and simple. They hate "darkies." Always have. (This is the classic South African explanation for why other people do what they do. Racism.)

During my time in Cape Town, I've seen expressions of all of these sentiments by coloureds towards Africans and the ANC: caution, anger, fear, racism.

But the explanation I find most persuasive is that the community felt a genuine anxiety about their status as a minority population going into a future where they would no longer enjoy the "relative privilege" that they had under white rule.

You see, during apartheid, despite being treated poorly, coloureds still enjoyed greater rights and opportunities than Africans. Though they were largely confined to menial jobs, they got preferential access to them through a job reservation policy which shielded them from competing with African laborers. And though they were forcibly removed from their homes to the soul-sapping townships of the Cape Flats, they were spared mass relocation to distant rural "homelands" that so many urban Africans endured.

This matters, this experience of relative privilege. It divides people, reducing the likelihood of solidarity amongst the oppressed. In Cape Town, this difference was compounded by the fact that coloureds came from a different historical and cultural background than Africans. Though both were subjugated by whites, coloureds had a different relationship to them by virtue of their social, linguistic, and cultural commonalities. And they did not have an automatic sense of kinship with Africans just because they were both "non-whites."

In many ways, the vote revealed that apartheid achieved some of its goals. It created enmity and distrust between people of different races. Physical divisions *and* mental ones. With the apartheid state's tight control of information and incessant propaganda, waves of negative stories about the ANC had been washing over coloureds for decades by the time they voted. They had been told that the ANC were "terrorists," that they couldn't be trusted, that they only cared for other Africans. Many coloureds took their wariness of the ANC into the ballot box.

Campaign differences were also key. The ANC assumed that coloureds would vote for it out of gratitude and self-interest. It did not do much to reach out to them in any specific way. In fact, many pundits at the time thought that the coloured identity would fade away as the "so-called coloureds" (as the more politically conscious South Africans liked to call them), would embrace a broader "black" identity in solidarity with Africans and Indians.

The National Party, on the other hand, targeted coloureds with racist *swart gevaar* (black fear) ads, stirring up worries that working-class coloureds would be overwhelmed by masses of African "migrants" from the Eastern Cape and neglected by "the black government." It touched a nerve. They also invited coloureds into the party, increasing their representation in the organization. While many educated and politically active coloureds voted for the ANC (which promised affirmative action, a policy that would greatly advance the long-suffering coloured middle class), the working-class majority threw its lot in with the Nats. That was enough for them to win the city and the province.

Since then, the "coloured vote" has been up for grabs. The National Party faded quickly and coloureds voted in greater numbers for the ANC, giving the party a chance to govern Cape Town and the Western Cape. But that didn't last either. They soon started voting for the DA which has been governing these parts for more than a decade. But the DA's hold on coloured voters is also tenuous: coloureds reevaluate their political options with frequency. This makes sense for a "middle minority" that—as coloureds love to say—"wasn't white enough in the past and isn't black enough in the present."

∿

That first democratic vote appears even more remarkable when we remember that the Nats were responsible for the greatest injustice of 20th century Cape Town: the forced removal of more than 150,000 Africans, coloureds and Indians from their homes in integrated neighborhoods to the bleak, distant townships of the Cape Flats. A grim feat of social engineering, the removals tore apart settled multi-racial communities and razed others to the ground. The comprehensive residential segregation that resulted remains the defining feature of Cape Town life today. A city fractured, racialized, unequal.

Between the late 1950s and early '80s, coloureds were moved to townships like Bonteheuwel, Heideveld, Manenberg, Bishop Lavis, and Mitchell's Plain. They were also sent to places with bucolic names like Lavender Hill, Hanover Park, Elsie's River, Beacon Valley, and Valhalla Park. They sound lovely, right? Hills, rivers, parks, valleys. A Norse paradise, even! Imagine being able to live in a place called Ocean View: you might even feel grateful to the government for sending you to such a place, based on the name.

If only it were so. For locals, the dissonance between what these words evoke in the abstract and the places they refer to in reality could not be more pronounced.

Indians were moved to Rylands in the Athlone area and Cravenby near Elsie's River. They were surrounded by coloureds, denoting their relative closeness to them in the apartheid hierarchy of races.

Africans, meanwhile, were sent to the scrublands beyond the coloured townships. They were dumped in Langa, Gugulethu, and Nyanga, all government-built "locations." But there were more people in these townships than could be housed, so they started expanding informal—"illegal"—settlements to places like Philippi and Crossroads. Eventually, through a mix of formal and informal development, Cape Town's largest African township, Khayelitsha, was established.

Essentially, Group Areas laws preserved the beautiful parts of town near the mountain and the beaches for whites, the sandy flatlands just beyond them for coloureds and Indians, and the blighted scrub beyond that for Africans. Concentric circles of hell emanating out from white nirvana.

But unlike in, say, India, where urban inequality is visible from every vantage point, where the poor live right next to the rich, Cape Town's racialized spaces are separated by *cordons sanitaires* like highways, train lines, industrial parks, golf courses, or conservation areas (see image 2). And the distances between these areas can be vast, such that a person who lives in the wealthier parts of the peninsula may never even step foot into a township during their entire lives. For them, the townships are places to avoid, to drive anxiously by on the freeway.

You can imagine what this leads to. The poor know very well how the wealthy live in Cape Town, as they travel into the leafy parts of the city for work or rec- reation. They carry back with them an intimate under- standing of how different their township world is from the whites'. They compare. They envy. They resent.

But the reverse is not the case. Middle- and upper- class Capetonians—white people especially—have very little knowledge of the world beyond their own suburbs. The Cape Flats, where most locals live, is terra incognita for them.

∿∿

When I first visited Cape Town in '97, I lived with a family in Mitchell's Plain, the largest (formerly) coloured township. This was so I could learn more about the coloured community. As I spent time with my neighbors there, I noticed that a lot of the older people would wax nostalgically about "the good old days" in places like District Six, Claremont, Sea Point, Simonstown, and other suburbs closer to the mountain. It sounded like they had read the *Buckingham Palace* book until I realized that, obviously, the book itself was an extension of these people's memories. They didn't need to read the book to lyricize their past: they had lived it.

What struck me was that, even though all of them had their own unique experiences growing up, they told their life stories in very similar ways. I wondered what it was that made their memories seem so connected, made them resonate with each other?

A few years later, as a graduate student of African Studies, I returned to the Cape to research the impact that Group Areas evictions had on victims' lives and memories. I interviewed over 100 removees who used to live in communities across the peninsula. One older woman from District Six, Mymoena Emjedi, shared biscuits and stories with me in her Bonteheuwel home, saying:

District Six was a wonderful place. There will never be a District Six like that anymore. In my street, there was different nations staying around. There was Africans, Indians, Europeans, Christians, Muslims, and we all grew up together. Everybody knew everybody.

We loved one another. But today you don't get people

like that anymore. Your neighbors now, they all live for themselves. They go past and don't even greet you. But in District Six, Christian people go "Good afternoon," and Muslim people say "Salaam aleikum" to one another. We could go out and not bother about our kiddies because the neighbors, they watch over them. Now the neighbors don't care for one another.

During Labarang, or Eid, which is like Christmas for Muslims, we would go to wish everybody well and the Christians would go wish with us. And when it's Christmas, then we go with them. And I can remember, when I was small, I would run away from home and sit in the mission with the Christian children and we would sing gospel songs together. You don't find that anymore.

We could walk till late at night through the streets. Nobody bothered you. You can go out in the summer, we can sit out on our stoeps (verandas) *outside...how can you do that here?! You've got to keep your doors locked everyday. There, in District Six, a girl can stay out from the morning till late night. I mean, OK, there were also corner boys in the streets, but they never bothered people. That was boys that helped old people get into buses, but not this type of gangs that grew up now.*

But when I was a teenager, I went out; I went to dance, I came home late in the evening. Street boys on the corner, they were all smoking, but not today's drugs, just dagga. *And they'd sit there and they'd sing on the corners. And you can sit the whole night on your stoeps and listen how they sing.*

When we grew up, our parents taught us to have

respect for the older. We used to go around and knock on elderly people's doors and ask them if they wanted anything from the shop. When we saw an elderly person getting in the bus, we would stand up for that person to come sit down. And if we go past an elderly person, we got to greet. But not today, the children walk past you. That respect is gone.

And that is why that time, there was no such crimes as they got here now, because today there's no more respect. Now, what is going to happen to the children one day when we not here? There's nobody to control them. When you go out, you see children sitting there smoking dagga, and around this corner, they're smoking drugs, and down the road you get a shebeen (illicit tavern). There's no decent future in this environment. If the government would have left us in District Six, then these crimes would not exist.

When we moved, we were very heartsore. We were kicked out of our family home that had been passed on from generation to generation. It was big, it had 7 rooms. But when they pushed us out, they scattered us all over. My brothers and sisters were sent to Steenberg, Hanover Park, Bishop Lavis, all over. I went to Heideveld and my mother had to go to Lavender Hill. My father died two weeks before we left though, in a car accident on the way home from a Jewish lawyer who he had hired to fight the government. My father said that he would never leave District Six, that they would have to carry him out. And it was true, just before we all had to leave, we did carry him, to his grave.

A poignant image of interracial harmony and its callous, unnecessary destruction. This is the Cape Town before Group Areas that exists in coloured removees' memories. Africans, Indians, coloureds, and "even that white people," coexisting in friendship, "like families." Where the interaction between the various races is remembered as tolerant, respectful, and mutually beneficial.

It is a portrait that is tenderly evoked, and with some pride. It is also asserted as a rebuke of the apartheid authorities' claim that different races were inherently antagonistic and would prosper more if they were segregated. In a city that is currently one of the most racially divided in South Africa, memories like this are especially striking.

After apartheid, many removees received token sums from the government for their ordeals while others have continued to demand an assisted return to their old neighborhoods. But most feel they will never get real justice or redress for this. It's not even possible, they say, considering what they lost.

Of course, many have now passed away, but their children carry their stories with them. Told wistfully, they lovingly recount the stories handed down to them. Stories about a patrimony that would have been theirs, if only. Stories about their connection to parts of the city beyond the townships. Stories you need to know to understand how Cape Town came to be the way it is today (see image 3).

Residential Inequality

District Six Life and its Destruction

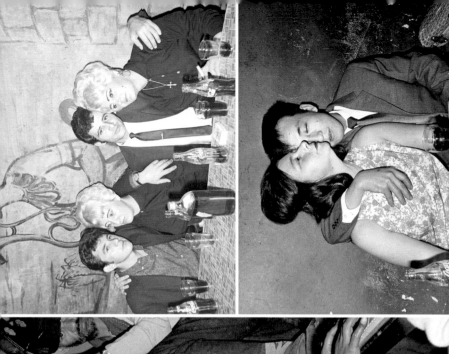

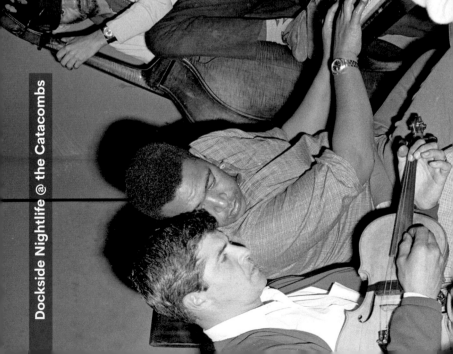

Dockside Nightlife @ the Catacombs

Minstrel in the Cape Town Minstrel Carnival

The Extended Bingham Family

Rhodes Must Fall Student Protests at UCT

Urban Art and Long Street

∿

Worker's Day, 1997. My girlfriend Marjorie and I step into a 3rd class train carriage at Lontogour station in Mitchell's Plain. She's just spent the afternoon with me and now I'm riding with her up to Maitland station, where she can catch a mini-bus taxi to her home in Factreton. The train is packed, full of families who've enjoyed a day at the beach. Marj and I lean against each other near the dual sliding doors which remain open as we ride, passengers' feet stopping them from closing.

As we pull out of the second station on the route, Nyanga Junction, a teenager runs alongside, jumping in and out of the train at our doors. Looks like he's just having fun. Seen it a hundred times. But as I'm about to zone out, I hear a hard snap and feel Marj's body flinch. She frantically looks around her. "My purse!" No one around us has moved, so I look for the kid who'd been running alongside the train. He's gone. He's yanked the bag off Marj's shoulder, then jumped off the train.

Before I can mutter, "That little shit just stole my girlfriend's purse," I follow him. I jump out of the train. I don't know if we are still next to the platform or next to a field or what. Nor do I consider the direction that the train is traveling. By the time I think of that, I'm already airborne. Thankfully I land on the platform— almost at its end—tumbling backwards when my feet touch the ground. I assume Marj will stay on the train and go home.

In a flash, I spring up like a cheetah, looking down the platform to see if I can spot the thief. Though hundreds of passengers have spilled out of the train, I can see a guy jogging down the platform, bobbing and weaving between the crowds. He doesn't look back. "The bastard thinks he's gotten away with it. I'll teach him!" I narrow my eyes and take off like a leopard.

I run as fast as I can, dodging the throngs along the way. But when I am about to catch the dastardly culprit, I wonder, "What would be the best technique to take this guy down?" I continue full speed and, as I tackle him from behind, I make sure his arms are pinned against his body so he won't be able to break his fall. Let the scumbag eat concrete!

With a mighty thump on the platform, he hits the deck and skids to a stop, with me on his back. Having immobilized him, I start to realize that it might look a little strange for a white guy to be randomly tackling a coloured guy at a township train station. So, as I turn him over, I yell, for all to hear, "Where's the purse?!"

The dazed kid stares back at me, startled, retorting, "What purse?!"

I stare back, brows starting to furrow. What purse, indeed. It wasn't in his hands. And I didn't see it fall to the ground when I tackled him. For the briefest of moments, I wonder whether I might have just face-planted a totally innocent guy. But then I shake that doubt out of my head, I confirm in my mind's eye that he was definitely the only one running. So it had to be him. But what if he passed the bag on to an accomplice along the way? Then I'm toast.

I grab him by his jacket lapels and shout again, "Where's the fucking purse?!"

He gives the same innocent response. And by this time, a crowd has circled us, enjoying the spectacle.

I pull open his jacket and, to my relief, there it is, nestled up against his body. I grab the bag, lift it high in vindication while leaning towards his face, "This purse, asshole!"

As I hold the bag triumphally aloft, I look up and see Marj standing right next to me! She'd jumped off the train straight after me, taking a tumble on the platform in her 5-inch heels. But then, like the cougar that she is (that's right, I said it—she's older than me—oh yeah!), she raced to my side.

I nonchalantly hand her the bag, like it was no big deal. Job done, I stand up and yank the jerk to his feet. I'm not quite sure what to do next. It's a public holiday. No cops to be seen. And I'm already quite pleased with how it's all turned out.

But the crowd wants more. Some chant, *"Moer hom! Moer hom!"* ("Kick his ass!"). I ponder it for a moment. But there was no point. And I wasn't sure I'd win a fight with this kid. We were on his home turf and he might be carrying a knife. I also later learned that he had a few accomplices in the crowd who were baying to get into the action. But their leader held them back, waiting to see what I'd do next.

But I can't leave the crowd hanging. So, summoning all my moral outrage, and with my finger pointed at the thief's face, I bellow, "And don't you EVER steal ANOTHER woman's purse again!" Then I shove him away, satisfied with myself. Oscar-worthy, that.

The crowd collectively groans and starts trudging away, bummed that nobody is going to get properly *moered*. Two old ladies clap in appreciation for my valiant defense of women's handbags.

The thief looks at me in disbelief as his mates start tugging him from behind, collecting him into their fold and jogging up the stairs out of the station. His pals laugh the whole way out, ribbing him for having been bested so dramatically.

∿

As you can imagine, I've told that story countless times at braais and cocktail parties, acting out all the various scenes. (I do the running and tackling sequences in slow-mo.) And while it's always nice to be the hero of one's own story, the underlying issue it deals with—the utterly commonplaceness of crime in Cape Town— doesn't usually lead to such humorous endings. It ends in tears, trauma or, even worse, death.

Some crime in the city is random and opportunistic, but a lot of it is organized, part of a broader criminal enterprise. And while the gangs that perpetrate so much of the city's crimes are based in the Cape Flats— where they are a scourge to their communities—their activities touch every part of the city. No one in Cape Town feels truly safe.

While gangsterism in the Cape certainly pre-dates apartheid, it was really through the massive social dislocations of the Group Areas removals that gang activity became prominent. The old protection racket of the Globe Gang in District Six was nothing compared to the organized syndicates that operate from the townships today. They're involved in everything from housebreaking, robbery, and murder to drug peddling, gun running, and abalone smuggling, to ATM heists, illegal betting and prostitution. In many areas, their shadow economy is simply *the* economy.

With colorful names like the Sexy Boys, Mongrels, Hard Livings, Americans, Brits, Scorpions, Laughing Boys, Nice Time Kids, Junior Mafia Syndicate, Clever Kids, and Thug Life, it is sometimes hard to imagine that guys who call themselves the Junky Funky Kids could be very dangerous. But don't be fooled. These playful names mask a more serious and sinister purpose.

Cape Town gangs come in various shapes and sizes. At the smallest and least formal level are *crews*. Street corner guys who run their own petty criminal activities (like stealing handbags from women on trains) and fight for small patches of turf with other crews. They're generally composed of kids from the same street or neighborhood, drawn in to protect each other from other kids. These are prevalent across the Cape Flats.

Then there are *cliques*, small groups of guys who prefer to operate in the shadows, but who often engage in quite violent activities, such as murder-for-hire, ATM heists, and carjacking. A lot of the taxi violence in the

African townships is executed through these cliques.

In the coloured townships are the famed *street gangs*, many of which can control broad swaths of area, though the exact delimitation of their territory is crucial to relations with neighboring gangs. Structured hierarchically with leaders, shot callers and soldiers, the function of these street gangs is primarily commercial. They make money through selling drugs—crystal meth (*tik*), *mandrax* (Quaaludes), marijuana, heroin—and other illicit schemes. A lot of that selling takes place in the townships, but gangs are connected to other enterprises that allow them to spread their merchandising, such as at nightclubs across the peninsula. They also develop relationships with police officers, politicians, and international crime syndicates. For many members, the money they make through the gang is their livelihood. It feeds their families.

Lastly, there are the infamous *Numbers gangs*—26s, 27s, 28s—that operate out of South African prisons. The numbers gangs sometime overlap activities with the street gangs, but their main focus is on internal prison management. Across Cape Town, you can't help but see these two-digit gang tags spray-painted on sundry buildings and signs. ("Slow for Pedestrian Crossing" *26!*)

The number of active gang members in the city is said to be over 100,000. Considering that Cape Town has the highest rates of murder, robbery, and property-related crimes in the country—along with a pervasive drug culture in the Cape Flats—the illicit drug-gang economy is a major engine of financial activities for many Capetonians and their dependents.

When I lived in Mitchell's Plain, the People Against Gangsterism and Drugs (PAGAD)—a vigilante self-defense organization—had just murdered the flamboyant head of the Hard Livings gang, Rashaad Staggie. Shot him in the head, then burnt him alive. After that, they attacked a number of other known drug dens with grenades and pistols. The gangsters were scared. So I actually felt pretty safe walking around, even late at night, in a township otherwise synonymous with gangsterism.

Later, though, when I lived in Bonteheuwel, some of PAGAD's members had gotten involved in jihadist activities, like bombing restaurants and pubs. Law enforcement put an end to that and PAGAD's influenced waned. So the gangs were operating out in the open again. I heard gun shots all the time, usually in the evening, after dusk. It was always unnerving trying to go to sleep to the crackling of gun fire.

The power, importance, and impact of the gangs goes up and down depending on several variables. Police effectiveness, drug supply, drug demand, the Rand exchange rate, formal job opportunities, internal gang dynamics, and so forth. But gangs themselves are a stable feature of township life. And they remain a menacing presence on the doorstep of the wealthier parts of town, occasionally prying those doors open—with crowbars—and taking whatever they like.

The fact that this threat has no boundaries was made

spectacularly clear when the leader of the Sexy Boys, Jerome "Donkey" Booysen, was targeted by rival gangsters in a hit at the Cape Town International Airport. Early morning in the drop-off zone, Booysen was shot four times, and a bystander was hit once as well. Both survived.

But the innocent are often not so lucky, becoming collateral damage in the endless feuding. At the beginning of 2017, in the space of just sixteen days, seventeen people were shot dead in Cape Town, many having nothing to do with gang activities.

One of them was Leslyn Mentor, a 26-year-old single mom from Lavender Hill who was returning to work for the first time since the birth of her daughter. She was a cashier at a nearby Pick-n-Pay supermarket. Taking an early morning taxi, she was killed when 13 bullets were sprayed through the taxi windshield by a gangster trying to kill the driver, himself a member of another gang. Leslyn and a fellow passenger died. The driver lived.

Such is life—and death—in a city precariously poised between first and third worlds.

BETWEEN EAST AND WEST

culture, style, identity

On my very first day in the Mother City in February 1997, I met my future wife. I had just arrived on an overnight train from Joburg, dropped my bags at a backpacker joint on Long Street, and moseyed down to the Waterfront on a warm summer Sunday afternoon. I walked into the first restaurant I saw. Black Steers Steakhouse. I ordered a Roquefort salad and took note of the beautiful lass waiting the tables opposite me.

Marjorie Bingham.

Working weekend shifts at the restaurant to help pay off her university loans. A second job, this, in addition to her full-time gig at a government office.

Hard-working. Intelligent. Childless. With all of her own teeth. I was smitten. I asked for a job on the spot.

Marjorie and I worked together as "waitrons" for a couple of months until Black Steers was bought out by Planet Hollywood and got bombed. Literally. From there, we started building the foundations of a lifelong relationship. Even despite the fact that her mom initially referred to me as a *fokken wit skollie*—fucking white thug—because I, a foreigner, had stolen her daughter's heart. (It's remarkable how perceptive Ma Bingham was, God rest her soul.)

Little did I know at the time, but our story was not unique. Like many other travelers, migrants, and sailors who had come before me to this vibrant port city, I found my bride at the water's edge.

After that first visit for six months, I returned to Cape Town a couple of times for academic research. For two years I lived with an older couple, Charlotte and Jones, in Bonteheuwel, a coloured township on the Cape Flats. These two epitomized the dockside culture that I had only gotten a small inkling of by hanging out at the Waterfront, but which I knew held the key to understanding this city.

Charlotte grew up near the docks in the Waterkant Street area with a dozen brothers and sisters. Some of the men in her family worked on the docks as stevedores, while her aunty next door entertained foreign sailors with a couple of other women. Charlotte grew up hearing the strange shanties of seamen who staggered around the neighborhood. She also heard the strange noises emanating from her auntie's *suikerhuisie* (brothel) next door.

Meanwhile, Jones was a primary school dropout who taught himself how to read while selling the *Cape Argus* newspaper on the street corner in District Six. In the evenings, he ran with a gang of petty warehouse thieves and street-lamp crooners called the Bun Boys. When he reached his teens, he worked on the docks with Charlotte's brother Joewa. Much to their boss' delight, they became proficient in stowing cargo—and much to their own, they became just as sharp at stealing it. Like longshoremen around the world, they always skimmed a bit of the passing trade.

Eventually, Jones got an engine-room job with Safmarine and traveled the world. During his four

decades at sea, he was hired and fired numerous times.
"Hard worker," his bosses would say. "But old school.
Always drinking." To which Jones would just shrug,
"Sometimes you've got to take the load off your mind."

When I lived with them, Charlotte and Jones told
me fascinating stories about Cape Town's port culture.
Through Charlotte I learned how females participated
in the maritime scene, largely as willing women ("port
hostesses") or waiting wives (raising families alone).
Through Jones, I gleaned the joys and tribulations of
the seaman's life, of adventure abroad and restlessness
at home. Their stories inspired me to look deeper into
Cape Town's dockside world.

∿∿

The people of these sailortowns like District Six provided labor for the entire shipping sector. Whole families
were engaged in servicing the maritime industry in one
way or another. They lived within sight of the harbor,
their eyes always seaward. The constant presence
of transient sailors had an impact on everyone in those
communities, as locals were constantly rubbing shoulders with foreigners. The very constitution of these
communities was bound up in maritime networks and
imagination.

The legendary township librarian and jazz musician,
Vincent Kolbe, liked to call himself a creole. An
Atlantico. He once told me that he felt more connected
to the people of Havana, New Orleans, Rio de

Janeiro and Southampton than to the landlubbers of Pretoria and Bloemfontein. That was because, when he was a young man and a budding pianist, he'd jam with international musicians in dockside joints like the Catacombs, where race didn't matter (see image 4). Growing up around District Six and the harbor, he learnt the value of transience, cosmopolitanism, hybridity, and improvisation. The dockside community stressed openness and interdependence.

But their outward-looking gaze went against the nationalist focus of apartheid. While Cape Town coloureds felt a sense of global connectivity, the white regime obsessed about land possession, ethnic rootedness, interior treks, and racial purity. It vaunted laager-style insularity as the metaphor for the nation, a circle of wagons to defend against others, not to connect with them. And it elevated blood and skin color as the arbiters of identity, not engagement or imagination.

Such claustrophobic nationalism rang hollow for Vincent because the maritime connections he grew up with were more important than the national bonds promoted by the up-country regime. Even way down at the southern tip of Africa, dockside communities were exposed to global ideological, cultural, genetic, and stylistic currents through passing seafarers. This mattered to their sense of identity and belonging in the world, the natural result of living at a global cultural intersection.

Thus the old docksiders were very cosmopolitan, not because they necessarily wanted to be so, nor because they were well-traveled, as most were not. But their constant interactions with foreign transients opened their minds to a world beyond South Africa.

∿

Nothing exemplifies Cape Town's intense trade in culture today better than the transactions that take place in its dockside nightclubs. Where local sugar girls cater to the sexual and recreational desires of foreign sailors.

Awhile back, I spent a year-and-a-half researching these relationships at dockside clubs, writing a book about them called *Sugar Girls & Seamen*. These nocturnal joints cater specifically to seafarers, offering them a place to drink alcohol, dance a bit, sing karaoke, shoot some pool, flirt with local girls, and then pay for their sexual services. Most of the guys who frequent these clubs are east Asian trawlermen from China, Vietnam, Indonesia, Korea, Taiwan, Japan, and The Philippines. Most speak very little English.

One evening at one of the clubs, I watched Renata —a coloured veteran who'd been in the game for years—enter the karaoke room quite late. The place was packed, but all the sailors were already busy with women. She skulked around a while, looking for an opening with a man. But with women draped around their shoulders, the men seemed content. Renata stood by the bar and listened to the seamen sing karaoke numbers for a while. Then she placed a request with the DJ.

When she took the microphone and stood in the middle of the room, no one noticed at first. It was fairly common for the women to sing too, usually American pop songs. But after she sang a few verses in flawless Mandarin, the men slowly turned their attention away from their women to Renata. The Chinese sailors gawked in amazement as Renata traversed the complex tones of a syrupy sweet ballad. The women wrapped their arms a little tighter around the men, burrowing their heads into the sailors' necks. But the men started singing along with Renata, encouraging her. Without missing a beat, she ramped up her performance, like a lounge singer from yesteryear. She glided around the tables with a sleek and sexy gait, sat on guys' laps, blew puckered kisses across the room and took command of the scene. For a few minutes, all eyes were on her.

When the song ended, everyone clapped and raised their glasses. The Chinese sailors were especially pleased. Their chests swelled to see this woman honor their culture with such a fine recital. They showered their praise on Renata, and for the rest of the evening she was welcome at any of their tables. The men fussed over her while the other women's faces started to sour.

The ploy paid off. At the end of the evening, Renata went off with a man who had been previously occupied with a woman who couldn't speak Chinese. Once his attention turned to Renata, it stayed on her.

As Renata departed with her beau, I stared at her, speechless. She was a 37-year-old coloured drug addict who slept between rock piles of the harbor breakwater at night—but she could speak, read, and write Chinese. And as the rest of the women went off with their men, I heard them chatting in the sailors' languages as well. I had to stop and ask myself, "Where the heck am I?"

Without a doubt, it is one of the most arresting images of the dockside scene: working-class coloured women singing karaoke in Chinese, seducing sailors in Taiwanese, negotiating sexual contracts in Korean, eavesdropping on conversations in Indonesian, cursing stingy salts in Tagalog, and cooing over companions in Japanese. They're such cunning linguists!

Indeed, from its earliest days, Cape Town has hosted —and been shaped by—not only indigenous Khoi and local Africans, but European migrants and settlers, Asian and African slaves and freemen, and a steady stream of seamen from all maritime nations. Located at the southern tip of Africa, yes, but also poised between east and west.

∿∿

While the dockside trade happens undercover, hidden from public view, there are many other rituals, practices, and events that reveal Cape Town's extensive traffic in culture—the most exuberant, iconic, ironic, and controversial expression of which is the Coon Carnival (aka the Cape Minstrel Carnival, aka the Kaapse Klopse). Take your pick.

It's an annual celebration of the coloured community's working-class heritage, connected in spirit to the diverse carnivalia of the post-emancipation world—like in New Orleans, Rio de Janeiro, and Trinidad and Tobago. It's where liberated blacks lay claim to their cities in colorful, noisy, physically animated spectacles.

Jones used to love reminiscing with me about his days of running with the minstrels in District Six and Woodstock. He'd get so excited describing how they'd practice song numbers in the months before the event, pay installments to the tailor for their outfits, march in town at the old Green Point Stadium, dance in the streets for the community, play homegrown *ghoema* music, and drink heavily throughout.

When I asked Jones if I could watch a club do some practices, he took me to Mitchell's Plain where people from his area of District Six had been forcibly removed. He introduced me to the Captain of the Lentegeur Entertainers who promptly invited me to join up.

So Jones and I went down to Lentegeur every week for the next months to practice. I was chosen to be one of the few of the three hundred-strong troupe to dance near the front, just behind the *voorlooper* (lead marcher) and *moffie* (drag queen mascot).

As a working-class amusement, the carnival caters to an annual boom/bust rhythmical cycle in which coloureds work hard for most of the year, and party just as hard at the end of it. The minstrel celebration is but one of a number of events on the summer festive season calendar for this community. In addition, there are also the Malay Choir competitions, *nagtroupe* performances, and Christmas Band parades. Many coloureds participate in more than one of these events.

A small number of Africans also contribute to the carnival. The people of Langa typically put forth a troupe of youngsters for the downtown street parade, though they do not compete for prizes at the stadium because they do not perform as minstrels, per se. They wear animal skin outfits that conform to a more rural and traditional cultural aesthetic, using the carnival as an opportunity to show off their unique heritage.

The carnival itself lasts four days as tens of thousands of minstrels march in dozens of troupes. On New Year's Day, they gather at their troupe Captain's house in the townships and sing and dance for the township audiences. They march up and down the streets, giving all the on-lookers a free show. They also linger at certain houses where they can expect a *tafel* (table) of food and drink for their efforts. Usually watermelon and local-brand soft drinks like Jive Cola. Older men often get some alcohol as well. They move on to other streets and other tafels. This lasts for hours.

Then they head to one of a number of stadiums across the city to compete for prizes in categories like: best uniform, best English comic song, best Afrikaans comic song, best juvenile song, etc. A team of judges patiently watches the endless procession of troupes perform. This goes on until after midnight in many cases. Then the troupes head to Bo-Kaap and finish the evening singing and dancing for the locals there.

On *Tweede Nuwe Jaar*, January 2nd, the troupes do it all again, but this time they also go to District Six and march through town, taking back the streets of the city which had been theirs for generations. This is the highlight of the carnival for most spectators and performers as thousands throng to watch the troupes dance by to the rhythms of the drums and trumpets. It is an awesome and colorful sight.

After this big day, the troupes meet again on the following two Saturdays to perform in the townships, compete at the stadiums, and croon away in Bo-Kaap, next to the city center. It's an exhausting and rewarding experience.

Troupes that win trophies enjoy massive prestige in their communities. Members strut with their heads held high, knowing that they've earned some serious bragging rights. It is this outcome, rather than the sentiments of random tourists who happen to glimpse their procession, which animates this carnival. The minstrels do all of this for themselves and their communities.

According to newspapers and carnival participants of the time, I was the first white person to ever run with the minstrels. The best headline I saw was, "This Yankee *mos* doodles like a dandy." Considering that this carnival had been going on for over a century, I was sure I wasn't the first white person ever, but perhaps the first in living memory. A sad testimony to how fractured race relations were made because of apartheid.

My future in-laws, however, were horrified I had joined. Even worse, they gasped when a newspaper article, showing me dancing in my blue and white satins, mentioned their precious daughter's name as my girlfriend. They felt so exposed! Like many other church-going, respectability-seeking coloureds, they saw the "coons" as an embarrassment. To them, it was a low-class parade of gangsters and hoodlums, good only to watch in guarded amusement from their stoeps, but never actually join.

Yet what has been nice to see since then is that more people of different backgrounds have started donning the satins. Though still rooted in the coloured townships, the carnival has become more cosmopolitan and female friendly. The number of women and girls has skyrocketed, bringing in a more family-centric vibe. The girls have also expanded the minstrel aesthetic to include the drum majorette look, derived from their own grade school experiences. And they have also broadened the likelihood that the faces on parade will not just be painted black (as was the norm in decades past), but in the green, purple, gold, neon or glittery silver colors of their outfits.

Of course, for Americans and Britons, the term "coon" rankles the senses. It is an offensive word, conjuring up degrading images of either whites putting on "blackface" or blacks doing the same, all for the sake of entertaining racist crowds in years gone by. But the term doesn't lead to such associations for the coloured working class. Why not?

Though the carnival traces its legacy back to the emancipation of slaves in the 1830s, the minstrel aesthetic derives from white and black American entertainers who brought the style to South Africa in the latter half of the 1800s. Black Americans were already considered cultural heroes for Africans and coloureds here, so whatever new styles or music they brought were often appropriated and remade for local tastes. This happened with spirituals back then and continues with jazz, gospel, R&B, hip-hop, fashion, and religious expression. So the minstrel aesthetic was taken up in Cape Town as a suitable way to pep up the annual procession celebrating the end of slavery.

Think about it. Black Americans have long been the coolest blacks in the world, certainly the ones that Cape coloureds have looked up to the most. Consider their similarities: both are descendants of slaves, have ancestry who were forcibly transported from far-away lands, have diverse genetic backgrounds, are minorities (around 10% of their national populations), speak European languages as their home tongues, and have never enjoyed political supremacy as a group in their countries. These similarities would have felt even more pronounced back in the late 1800s, promoting a sense of identification.

Over time, the "coon" aesthetic lost its appeal in America and Britain, symbolizing a history of oppression and humiliation by whites against blacks. But in Cape Town, because it was appropriated by working-class coloureds and performed for their own amusement, it never took on such negative meanings for them. Rather, the idea of the coon remained rather apolitical, a symbol of New Years' revelry and *jolling*.

The term is a reminder that the globalization of ideas has been going on for a very long time. In Cape Town, the "coon" is just another—admittedly controversial and provocative—historical cultural artifact (see image 5).

∿∿

Cape people, half-castes, white *Kaffirs*, God's step-children, *Bastards, Hottentots*, Eurafricans, half-breeds, racial hybrids, middle minority, buffer group, mixed-bloods, marginal men, in-betweeners, brown Afrikaners, middle children, twilight people, blacks, so-called Coloureds, people of mixed race, *Camissa, kleurlings, bruinmense, Boesmans, gam*: just a few names given through history to the people now called—and who call themselves—coloureds.

This sprawling (and mostly offensive) nomenclature reveals South Africans' uncertainty concerning how to understand people whose genetic and cultural diversity resists narrow racial categorization. In fact, in apartheid law, coloureds were literally deemed those who were not "obviously" African, European, or Indian. They were a reservoir category, a collection of people who did not conform to the purist racial fantasies of white men.

Indeed, the genetic range of this community is staggering. Recently, my wife and I took DNA tests to learn more about where our ancestors came from. My results confirmed my deepest fears—that all my

forbears were European immigrants who settled exclu-
sively in the southern states of the US, thereby making
me 100% Redneck. (Yee-haw!)

But my wife's results were almost comically kalei-
doscopic, exemplifying the complicated genetic and
cultural heritage of Cape coloureds.

According to her test—which should be taken with
a pinch of salt, given the speculative nature of some of
the methodology—43% of Marj's ancestors are *African*.
Namely Khoisan, Bantu and West African. The high
proportion of Khoisan was expected, given the history of the region. The presence of Southern African
Bantu (like Xhosa or Tswana) was also unsurprising,
given their long history of interacting with the Khoisan.
The smaller West African contribution was curious, but
helped substantiate family stories that some ancestors came from St Helena island, a British possession
that historically hosted numerous Atlantic nationalities,
including West Africans.

Next, 34% of Marj's ancestors are *European*, mostly
of English and Welsh heritage, with some Scandinavian
in there too. With a surname like Bingham, the British
connection was assumed, now confirmed. The
Scandinavian contribution (7%) is likely explained by
the fact that British people carry a lot of Scandinavian
genetic markers themselves, due to the long history
of Viking incursion and settlement in Britain. But more
curiously, there was no mention of "Northern European"
in her results, meaning there were no apparent Dutch
or Afrikaner markers in the mix.

Lastly, 18% of Marj's ancestry are *Asian*. The majority (10%) are of Indonesian extract and slightly less (7%) Indian. Given the direct connections between Indonesia and the Cape via the Dutch, this made sense. While Cape Muslims more often identify with their Indonesian heritage, this result shows that coloureds of all faiths may bear traces of those distant islands as well. The smaller Indian presence may have to do with interactions with local Indians, but we think it goes back to St Helena, where numerous Indians spent time during the colonial era, and some of whose descendants migrated to Cape Town.

So, there it is. One person's ancestral traces from the Cape coloured community (see image 6). An impressive array of genetic influences, for sure, but not even close to the magnitude of diversity that comprises the broader coloured population.

You might be thinking: "Wow, these people can claim such a varied inheritance! Khoisan, Bantu, Asian, European, you name it! They can pick and choose which legacies they want to emphasize in their lives, right?!"

No.

Because the coloured identity is essentially premised on them *not* being African, Indian, or European, this has made it almost impossible for coloureds to claim or emphasize these backgrounds. Local African, Indian, and white populations would be puzzled by their claims while other coloureds would think them delusional for trying to disaggregate their complex lineage.

In fact, this dizzying diversity has made it more practical for most coloureds to just think that any such ethnogenesis begins with "other" racial groups "mixing" in the Cape during colonialism, thereby creating a new people. This understanding helps connect coloureds together, as the specifics of their mixed backgrounds matter less than the simple fact of their mixedness. But it also flattens their rich genealogical heritages down to a dull racist formula: if not "pure" African, Indian, or European, then coloured.

Bizarre. But, what can you do?

Well, some activists have tried to rally coloureds around a Khoisan identity, as indigeneity can provide powerful moral and political claims in certain contexts. The Khoisan, in some ways, can be considered the "original" South Africans, so that should make coloureds feel proud of their heritage, and demand greater recognition for their own rights as "Africans." But few coloureds have taken up the cause.

For many, there remains a taint around their Khoisan roots because whites so denigrated these indigenes in the past that coloureds felt ashamed to recognize them as ancestors. In fact, especially in years past, coloureds tried to de-emphasize any connection to them by straightening their hair, marrying light-skinned partners, bleaching their skin, and doing anything they could to approximate white standards. These were the actions of a vulnerable community trying to survive white supremacy. Awkward stuff was bound to happen. (Heck, it still does.)

Other activists have tried to elevate the importance of coloureds' slave heritage, encouraging them to take pride in their ancestors who managed to survive their wretched situation and still bequeath to them a vital legacy. African-Americans have done this in the US, and it has elevated the sense of pride they have in their history. But in Cape Town, the remoteness of that period, and the fact that the horrors of apartheid have basically usurped the moral power of slavery-based political and identity claims, has made it a hard sell for Cape coloureds.

But there are reminders of that slave history every-where, especially in the surnames of coloureds them-selves. Many families have last names like January, February, April, August, and September, derived from the month that one of their slave ancestors arrived by ship. Some were given names from Greek and Roman mythology like Adonis, Apollis, or Cupido. (I'm not sure why.)

But most common are surnames taken from the Biblical first name of an ancestor's slaveowner—Abraham, Isaac, Jacob, Paul—combined with the Afrikaans possessive ("s" or "se") after it. Hence: Abrahamse, Isaacs, Jacobs, Paulse. These surnames resulted from the question: "Whose slave are you?" "I'm Abraham's." Abrahamse. And just like that, a history of violence and possession was inscribed into the names of future generations (though most who bear these names are unaware of this history).

Of course, there are plenty of exceptions to South

Africa's peculiar racial rules. During apartheid, many African Capetonians reclassified as coloureds to get better access to jobs, goods, and services. They took coloured surnames and improved their Afrikaans, all in an attempt to game an effed-up system. Light-skinned coloureds also reclassified themselves—or just casually passed—as white to gain a step up in the racial hierarchy. White people who married coloureds were also forced to be reclassified as coloureds if they wanted to remain married and live with their families in designated "coloured areas."

Today, while the coloured identity remains open to anyone "mixed," those born of such unions today (first-generation, so to speak) are not automatically considered coloureds. They can claim this identity if they want, but most now feel that individuals should be allowed "more" freedom in choosing their own identities, especially if they align with one of the parent's backgrounds.

In sum, the Cape coloured community's unique genetic make-up, cultural heritage, and racial iden-tity means that, while they are no doubt indigenous to Africa, they're not seen as African. And though they are clearly Westernized, they're not seen as Westerners. Shaped by all, claimed by none. Leaving them with the one name they can truly call their own: *Kaapenaars*.

This lengthy discussion of coloured history, culture, and

ancestry might seem odd given that, at a national level, it is the relationship between Africans and whites that has mattered the most in this country. It is these two groups that have produced the dramatic, wrenching dynamics shaping this country's recent past.

And while there are many Africans and whites in Cape Town, it can be difficult at times to elaborate what their respective cultures might amount to. Because, unlike Cape coloureds, whose culture is rooted not only in this very specific peninsular ecology and in the cosmopolitan interactions with itinerant sailors over centuries, Africans and whites have brought cultural elements from further afield to this city. And they still do.

Both have ancestral homes elsewhere where the foundations of their cultural identities and practices emerged. Though some may have only a tenuous, or non-existent, relationship to those places now, their histories emanating from other places matter deeply to how they think of themselves today in the Cape. They too are cultural in-betweeners like the coloureds, but in a different way.

Thus most Africans in the city enjoy an abiding relationship with the Eastern Cape, the neighboring province some hundreds of miles eastward of Cape Town. They are mostly Xhosa people whose ancestors, culture, and heritage are rooted in the hills and valleys of that land. Though many have been in Cape Town for generations, and may not have much to do with the Eastern Cape in a practical sense, the vast majority draw continued cultural inspiration from that region.

And indeed, most have direct ties to it, spending portions of each year visiting family there. (They also closely follow trends and developments in Joburg, the epicenter of black urban life in SA.)

A number of their cultural practices that often seem striking in this urban landscape come straight from their rural heritage. Some continue to herd livestock on the fringes of the townships, with their beasts forming an occasional traffic jam for impatient drivers. They do their best to reproduce the manhood-transmission ritual of *ulwaluko*, in which teenage male initiates spend time in the "bush" (such as it is in this crowded metropolis) with their elders, wearing only blankets and a thin smearing of white clay, earning adult status with the cut of a circumciser's blade. (Ouch!) They also try to ensure that *lobola* (bride price) negotiations form part of any nuptials, modifying them to suit their modern, urban context. And, for big occasions, many still prefer to slaughter animals themselves rather than buying pre-cut meat from the butcher, as it is in the killing itself that a ritual, ceremony, or feast takes on deeper significance.

In addition, there remains a rural sensibility to the type of social engagement animating African townships. That is, despite the massive density of these areas, the throngs of pedestrians, merchants, and drivers on the streets interact with each other in a spirited, open manner (unlike in the crowded cities of the US, where people don't even look at each other). The streets are alive, transactional, vital. This conviviality emerges from the high-trust rural cultures that continue to inspire urban Africans, though they are constantly adapting this to suit present circumstances.

The picture is a bit different for white Capetonians. Anglos continue to have a cultural and emotional connection to Britain, even if they do not all have direct personal ties anymore. Many of them derive from ancestors who lived modest lives in the UK decades or centuries earlier, then sailed abroad for a better life. They were part of an extensive migration of Brits to colonies around the globe. But they brought their culture with them and, as much as possible, tried to replicate and propagate their values once re-settled. (Think America, Australia, Canada, and New Zealand. All multi-cultural countries dominated by Anglo cultural sensibilities.) In Cape Town, their cultural influence remains powerful, shaping almost every area of civic life, expressed religiously through Anglicanism, politically through liberalism, philosophically through secularism, socially through paternalism, and linguistically through English.

And while Anglos' accents, surnames, and approach to life also mark them as sharing a common heritage and connection to Britain, that relationship is more muted now, so the South African side of their identity has grown more pronounced. But it still matters, especially in a mental and emotional sense.

This Anglo cultural sensibility is experienced most powerfully at the institutional level. Even though Anglos don't necessarily assert their connections to the UK with literal travel, many of Cape Town's most powerful businesses, organizations, and academies try to mimic the standards set in Britain for guiding their own practices. For these institutions, prestige and excellence is often simply based on how closely they resemble some counterpart in the UK.

When I started working at the University of Cape Town (UCT), a traditional Anglo institution, the leadership revealed a slightly troubling need to be acknowledged by British university rankings boards. Improving their status in these rankings justified virtually everything they did. I didn't quite get this need for British recognition, but if I'm cynical, I can see how such appeals to British "standards" helps them maintain a high level of cultural and economic power here. If the yardstick of institutional excellence emanates from British exemplars, then individual Anglos here can maintain a lot of their prestige and importance just by being themselves. By reproducing Anglo cultural norms in the institutions where they study or work—and where people of other backgrounds must also prove themselves—they are able to set rules that end up privileging their own preferences and practices.

This is no different than the approach taken by other Anglo communities around the world, but it means they rarely end up gaining a deep knowledge of other cultures or foreign languages. They travel in circles which promote English as the standard of communication and remain insulated from needing to accommodate themselves to non-Anglo mores. They may engage with people from other backgrounds in daily life, especially in hierarchical service situations, but the limits of such interactions are clear.

I say all of this with more understanding and complicity than I'd like to admit. After all, I'm a card-carrying member of the tribe myself, from the 'Merican clan. And while my people might be unrefined (chanting "U-S-A! U-S-A!" whenever we meet) compared to the polished Anglos here, we bear an equally arrogant presumption that others should make themselves acquainted with our ways, not us with theirs. It's a luxury we've derived from long histories of imperialist expansion.

Afrikaners, on the other hand, lost any meaningful connection to their European "home" once the British took over the Cape. Trekking deep into the interior in the 1830s, Afrikaners cut themselves off by-and-large from European intellectual and cultural trends, developing their own unique culture in response to the region's challenging ecological and social environment. Their language was simplified from Dutch to Afrikaans as they interacted with non-Dutch speakers who were central to their domestic economies: slave and Khoisan subordinates.

Their lives in the interior could not have been more different than the ones their ancestors would have had in Europe, making it less necessary for them to tap into that well of memory. The world that they forged upcountry in the Orange Free State and Transvaal became the key sites of their ethnic identification and volk-building. Full of dramatic military engagements against African warriors and British soldiers, the Afrikaners staked their claim to this southern land and forsook all others. The Netherlands features little in Afrikaners' sense of identity today. It is the African interior that looms largest in their history. (This is similar for the majority of Americans who root their sense of identity in relatively recent history, focusing on the moments *after* their ancestors migrated to, or were enslaved in, the US.)

Because the highveld has had such a powerful impact on Afrikanerdom, they have actually adopted a number of similarities to the African peoples they encountered. They are deeply attached to land as a concept, to "the soil." They revere livestock herding and ranching, similar to their African neighbors. They have a history of deep religious belief and continue to promote some variation of patriarchal domesticity. And they anchor much of their ethnic pride in machismo-based displays, especially their men's prowess on the rugby pitch, with the Springboks acting as a kind of barometer on the standing of Afrikaners in this country. (Even Mandela recognized this. His enthusiastic support for the 1995 Springboks at the Rugby World Cup created a lasting emotional impact on Afrikaners who had been anxious about their place in post-apartheid South Africa. Immortalized in the movie *Invictus*, his donning of the green and gold jersey let Afrikaners know that he acknowledged them and their culture.)

In Cape Town, Afrikaners draw inspiration from this upcountry history, but integrate it with their urban reality. The parks of their neighborhoods in the city's

northern suburbs—where many live today—have
playgrounds with ox wagon jungle gyms, so their kids
can recreate the Great Trek. The names of many of
the streets there refer to male Afrikaner heroes who
made their names in battle or politics. And, despite
the growing predominance of English as the connecting language between South Africans, they continue
to speak, pass on, and invest in the language that is
central to their identity. A language named after themselves and the continent to which they claim belonging: Afrikaans.

Indeed, if this book were about South Africa rather
than Cape Town, I would focus a lot more on Afrikaners.
Nationally, they have made a far deeper cultural imprint
than Anglos. And while such a book would reveal much
that is to be admired about Afrikaners' cultural ingenuity
and resilience, we'd also find much to critique and
lament. We'd have to reckon with the centrality of
slavery and apartheid to Afrikaners' history, culture,
and identity (just as I and other Americans have to in
understanding the legacy of our ancestors in the US
South).

Meanwhile, Indians in Cape Town also enjoy deep
connectivity to Indians elsewhere, primarily in Durban,
and to a lesser extent Joburg and India. Durban Indians
are considered the prototypical South African "Indian,"
so the small community in Cape Town is able to refresh
its cultural resources through a selective borrowing of
ideas and developments in Durban. The fact that most
Cape Town Indians are middle or upper class does

mean, however, that they are less interested in what happens in Durban's substantial working-class Indian community.

More recently, though, the elevation of India on the global stage has meant that many now find inspiration directly from their ancestral homeland. Some travel there for tourist adventures or meet up with distant relatives. Such experiences can, ironically, reinforce just how South African they actually are—and prefer to be—because of how different life is in Cape Town compared to India. But they can pick and choose what they like from the exposure, adding to their culinary education, artistic and design inspirations, and especially cinematic enjoyment with the plethora of Bollywood films now on offer everywhere.

Lastly, many other smaller Burundian, Chinese, Congolese, Nigerian, Somali, and Zimbabwean communities live here and maintain strong connections to families back in their home countries, often remitting money to them. Pretty quickly, though, they have had to accommodate themselves to the more established cultures of Cape Town, learning how to navigate them for survival and prosperity. That has not always been easy though, as many have been targeted in deadly xenophobic attacks by poorer Capetonians who resent their presence. But over time, as they settle down, their migrant status typically fades and they become "local," similar to the Greeks, Portuguese, and Lithuanian Jews, all former migrant communities that have since been folded into the city's (white) population.

All of this is just to say that, except for coloureds whose culture was developed in the greater Cape Town area (though also drawing on myriad sources beyond), Africans, whites, Indians, and other communities often continue to draw cultural inspiration from ethnic origin sites elsewhere that are considered more central to their specific identities than that of Cape Town itself.

This matters because, even in such a mixed, cosmopolitan city like this, different ethnic groups continue to draw on cultural resources from within and without. These communities interrogate their understandings of themselves in relation to what is happening in the places that gave birth to and nurtured their ancestors. In some cases, Capetonians feel replenished by this engagement; in others, repulsed, as they diverge in their values or practices from their distant ethnic kin.

And that's what makes this city such a fascinating cauldron of culture. Between east and west, north and south, Africa and the world.

BETWEEN PAST AND FUTURE
transformation, aspiration, belonging

Recently, black students at the University of Cape Town (UCT) started calling for radical changes at the country's premier institution of higher education. They argued that the curriculum needs to be "decolonized," to move away from its Eurocentric approach to knowledge, teaching, and learning. They urged greater diversity in the faculty members who teach them, so that students can learn from people who come from similar backgrounds as themselves. And they demanded greater black representation in the faculty Senate which governs the direction the university takes, as it was largely made up of older white males.

The university responded by saying that there were proper protocols that had to be heeded. That changes to the curriculum needed to follow certain processes and procedures. That, though the university was trying to hire more black faculty members, those who met UCT's exacting standards often chose to work elsewhere, especially in the private sector where they could earn higher salaries. And the Senate? Well, only full professors automatically qualified to become members, so the handful of younger black faculty members at UCT would struggle to gain access in real numbers anytime soon.

Protocols, procedures, processes, standards. These are the words that liberals love. They represent order, indeed Civilization itself. But more strategically, they

also act as a lexical bulwark behind which the beneficiaries of Anglo cultural hegemony can safely retreat
when The Excluded start pressing for changes that
would directly affect them

In contexts of relative equality, diversity, and opportunity, these words are fine. They maximize quality,
fairness, and consistency. But at UCT, these words im-
pede black transformation and belonging. They hinder
the educational outcomes that the university otherwise
seeks to achieve.

The students figured this out fairly quickly, realizing
that there would be no meaningful changes made so
long as the terms of the discussion focused on adminis-
trative rules and regulations. So they shifted the debate
to history, identity, and justice. Terrain where the poor
have much greater leverage.

They did so by attacking a symbol that is synonymous
with white racism, one that is deeply tied to Cape Town
and UCT. An indefensible symbol whose name connotes
both educational prestige and colonial domination:
Cecil John Rhodes. British diamond magnate, iconic
scholarship giver, and high priest of Anglo imperialism.

Coordinating their protest through the hashtag
#RhodesMustFall, the students laid siege to a brooding
Rhodes "thinker" statue at the center of campus. They
vandalized it with graffiti, urine, and feces, demanding
its removal. And they felt their collective strength grow
as they rallied, day after day, against the administration and its security personnel.

For these students, Rhodes might have been long

dead, but his spirit seemed to live on in the institutional ethos of Anglo superiority, the imperial smugness that the university appeared to be founded upon (sited so as to gaze over "Africa"), and the patriarchal entitlement that masculinity and seniority ensured in its structures.

As one of the protest leaders, Chumani Maxwele (who was also a leader in the Clifton beach protests), stated, "My institution celebrates this man [Rhodes]. At UCT you have all signs of symbols which celebrate white structure...all signs of celebration are there before you, my black brother, but nothing about you is being celebrated."

Most UCT staff, of course, disavow any connection to Rhodes or what he represents. But they couldn't help but understand that the protest wasn't "really" about Rhodes, or a history that no one can change. It was about *them*. It was about the present. It was about how they, as the custodians of UCT (built on land "given" by Rhodes), are the ones now responsible for holding back black advancement at the university. It was about how they, wittingly or not, were carrying on Rhodes' legacy by not acting quickly and decisively on the issue of black inclusion.

Having worked at UCT for some years myself, I can attest that most of the people I know there are politically progressive, with a keen desire to uplift South African students. And yet, they operate within an institution where even well-meaning attitudes, actions, and decisions can lead to exclusionary outcomes because they are structured by processes that are inherently conservative. They—I—continue to benefit from institutional bias. And thus, the university once known as "Moscow on the Hill" for its radicalism during apartheid Is, Ironically, one of the loact racially transformed educational institutions in the country today.

The protest made this point very clearly. And it made many people who would have initially thought they weren't implicated by such protests very uncomfortable. In grappling with the deeper symbolism of the anti-Rhodes movement, many had to face troubling truths about identity, history, and power.

While the original goals of the movement—regarding curriculum, diversity, and governance—remain issues that will take some time to change, the students succeeded in making these matters of urgency across all faculties.

More immediately, the students were able to force the administration to remove the Rhodes statue. A powerful moment, that, as the crane hoisted Rhodes off his pedestal and dumped him into the back of a truck for transport to a distant warehouse (see image 7).

Emboldened by this, the students then channeled their energies into the larger #FeesMustFall movement which was being organized by students at every university across the country. Demanding free tertiary education for all, their protests led to lengthy campus shut-downs, property damage, and the postponement of final exams. More importantly, their militant action pressured the government to abolish higher education fees for students from poorer backgrounds. This was the first—though likely not the last—protest victory of these young hashtag radicals.

Capetonians. Between a stubborn past and an impossible future.

∿

A few years ago, local academics published a report on African workers' and professionals' perception of "transformation" (black inclusion through affirmative action) in the Western Cape. It quotes a number of residents who said that they did not feel transformation was positively influencing their life chances here. Compared to cities like Joburg, they felt that "they often face a monolithic and exclusionary environment in which they are made to feel unwelcome." The conclusion of the study was that "there was a broad consensus that Cape Town is hostile to African people."

A *Cape Times* headline put it bluntly, "Cape Town a racist city—study."

When I read the report, it didn't strike me as very controversial. Given the city's history and demography, should it be a surprise that Africans might find the city less hospitable than others?

Yet the leader of the DA and Premier of the Western Cape, Helen Zille, blasted the report as a political hit job, saying that "those who accuse the entire City or Province of racism are themselves racist." (The old "I know you are, but what am I" defense.) She asked, "If Cape Town is racist, why are people moving to the City in such significant numbers?" The report was dismissed as "racial propaganda."

The DA's prickly response to a report that never mentions it—or even party politics at all—suggests that it felt implicated in the judgments that Africans were making about the Cape. It took their critique of the province and the city as an indictment of the party.

Yet that was not what African residents were saying here. Their dissatisfaction with transformation in the Cape had more to do with cultural challenges at the workplace, language issues, continued residential segregation, and their comparatively better experiences in other African-majority cities.

This same sentiment has been echoed by other African professionals ever since, that "Being in Cape Town feels like being in another country. Cape Town is cliquey, unAfrican, unwelcoming."

The feelings that these workers and professionals were sharing go deep. After all, Africans have a long history of feeling unwelcome in South Africa. In 1913, the Native Lands Act confined their right to land ownership to just 13% of the land. Marginal scrub, for the most part. During apartheid, they were forcibly relocated from the cities to rural Bantustans—"independent countries," as the regime liked to call them—made to feel as if they were foreigners in their natal land. And much of the Cape Province was a labor preference zone for coloureds, minimizing Africans' economic opportunities in Cape Town. This stuff has been going on for a long time. Africans were just saying that this legacy hasn't completely gone away.

∿

Up until recently, the concerns shared by African Capetonians were issued from the position of relative poverty. Their demands centered around basic service provision such as running water, sanitary toilet facilities, electricity access, and affordable housing. But with the community's notable educational, professional, and financial growth since the end of apartheid, African voices are now being asserted not only in the streets, but in the boardroom as well. It is one of the biggest changes that is currently re-shaping social relations in Cape Town today: the growth of an African middle-class which has the power to influence consumer trends, educational curricula, political campaigns, and social justice strategies.

The emerging African middle class in Cape Town is made up largely of educated professionals, some of whom had their formative years under apartheid, and some who were born after liberation (the "Born Frees"). This has created a fascinating debate between them about how they should engage with the state, and how they should continue to try to transform the private sector so that Africans have better opportunities.

The middle-aged members of this group tend to have a long-term, comparative understanding of their situation. With few options during apartheid, they remain grateful for the changes wrought by 1994. They were able to take advantage of the openings that emerged and gradually build themselves up to a comfortable standard of living. They are not satisfied with the slow manner in which black advancement has taken place in the private sector in Cape Town, but their style has been one more of patient persistence than open confrontation in pushing for change. These are people who are propertied, insured, and with offspring: they have a lot to lose if they rock the boat too hard.

The younger Born Frees, on the other hand, do not feel beholden to the social and ethical mores of struggle history. They look beyond the political battle (which has already been won) to the more subtle economic and social forces shaping their lives. This is their generation's battle. They take for granted their political liberty and seek to enjoy all of the social, recreational, and financial opportunities that should flow from such freedom. They are social media mavens, consumer capitalists, and Afropolitan in their outlook: open to the world, but with a keen eye on black art, music, literature, and fashion. They can also be iconoclastic, like youth anywhere in the world.

Critics of this younger generation say that they act entitled, impatient and, sometimes, disrespectful. By focusing so squarely on their own current concerns, they appear to be dismissive of the sacrifices made by their forebears. Indeed, some of the more provocative Born Frees have even suggested that their elders did not do enough to secure their future prosperity (a charge which incenses people over a certain age).

This is a complex inter-generational discussion, but I'd like to reframe the Born Free perspective in a way that makes their "impatient," "entitled" claims easier to understand. Think of the Born Frees—and all historically underprivileged people—like shareholders in a collective national corporation. When they demand more services, resources, and opportunities, they are demanding no more and no less than what they believe is due to them from this bountiful country. They're demanding this as equals with other shareholders, especially whites (who used to control most of the shares, so to speak). This demand is made from the position of having—not still clamoring for—rights.

While the Born Frees' parents might have secured their rights, they are the ones insisting that these rights have practical social and economic outcomes. As national shareholders, they have every right to cash in that share when they please: and they want to do it now, thank you very much.

Of course, there are endless difficulties in the state delivering on those claims, and that is frustrating for claimants. Even more frustrating for upwardly mobile blacks is that, unlike their elders who faced off against a recognizable foe in the apartheid government, the social and economic challenges facing them are more diffuse, harder to confront directly.

While blacks enjoy full legal access to any profession they desire, they find that the unspoken norms and practices—all of which were developed prior to liberation by white males—actually govern whether they can get very far in those fields. They can get entry level jobs based on their educational qualifications, but no matter how hard they work, many struggle to advance to the higher echelons of management and ownership where real money, power, and influence lies. Where aspiration meets actualization.

I learned this from my wife. Marjorie grew up during apartheid and, after matriculating from high school, got a job in the Surveyor General's Office in the Department of Land Affairs. As a clerk there, she dealt with attorneys who'd come in to ask for property maps and info. In her evenings, she studied for a Bachelor's in psychology and sociology at the University of the Western Cape (to her parents' dismay, as they thought she should have been satisfied with her "fancy" office job).

But after '94, Marj decided she wanted to stand on the other side of the counter: as a property attorney. So she went back to UWC and got a law degree. After passing the bar, she was hired by a big firm, the fulfillment of a dream. Life in the New South Africa looked bright for her.

But over time, as she fantasized about moving up the ranks and someday becoming a partner at her firm, she began to see how her background and education did not prepare her for such an ascent. She had the technical capacity to do the legal work set before her, but she lacked the one thing that really mattered for advancement: wealthy, inherited social networks.

At the big firms of almost every profession in Cape Town, many blacks find that it is not competency, integrity, or hard work that brings meaningful advancement, but having social connections with high net worth individuals who can be brought in as clients. These personal relationships are the key not only to the financial health of the firm, but also to the prospects of the people who bring them in.

Like most of her black colleagues, Marj lacked organic access to high-wealth networks which, in this city, center largely around the alumni of elite boys' academies. These are former all-white schools where young white men have, for decades, forged high-trust bonds that have utility far beyond the schooling years. Because they are developed during adolescence, they remain durable over time, allowing members to casually merge the worlds of business and pleasure in adulthood as they hang out on golf courses or wine estates, chatting business and striking deals.

(Compare that with Marj's educational experience. During the 1986 State of Emergency, when the country was on lockdown and armored police carriers were patrolling the townships, her teachers were sending her to the corner shop to buy them cigarettes. She shakes her head when she thinks about it: "While white students were learning how to rule the world, I was fetching packets of Rothman's Blue for my teachers. All part of my 'gutter education.'")

Obviously, Marj's township social networks didn't have much financial value to her firm, so she reached out to big players, especially developers and property tycoons. But even though they were always polite with her, it was easier for them to stay with the male attorneys they already knew through prior social connections. In the end, after enough of these "polite" but fruitless interactions, she struck out on her own and started her own boutique firm, which she has been running for the last decade.

It's a common story in this field. Start at a big firm, then when you bump into the glass ceiling, become a sole practitioner where you get to be your own boss, yet have very little influence within the profession. (And make less money while taking on more responsibility.)

Of course, one could shrug and say that this is just how it is: big firms need lots of revenue to thrive. Attorneys must bring in their own high-value clients if they want to be promoted. There's nothing overtly discriminatory in all of this.

But because of this city's past, this arrangement drastically privileges white males over everyone else. Since many enjoy taken-for-granted access to high-net-worth individuals, they don't have to work hard to entice them as clients, except in competing against other white men to secure them.

This helps us understand why, even though 46% of the country's legal profession is made up of women, two-thirds of attorney's practices are owned by men and 80% are owned by whites. Black female access to the field has not changed the economic and power dynamics ensuring white male dominance.

On top of that, black female professionals also face a more insidious obstacle to their career aspirations:

doubt. Doubt from others, doubt from themselves. Lwando Xaso, a young attorney practicing commercial law at one of the most prestigious firms in Cape Town, says that it is "common for black women to feel compelled to work longer hours in order to disprove the stereotype that black women have a poor work ethic. However, working long hours can reinforce another stereotype that black women need more time to complete a task that would take someone else half the time." A Catch-22.

With the constant stress that accompanies such work, she soberly concludes, "I do not know of any black woman attorney who will retire as a lawyer at a firm."

That's right, despite the entrance of so many blacks and women to the legal profession, white males remain securely in control of the real wealth, opportunities, and direction of the law and many other professional sectors in Cape Town.

This isn't the liberation dividend that blacks expected from being shareholders in this great country.

∿∿

Ironically, it could be argued that whites have been the greatest beneficiaries of the liberation dividend. They were able to keep their wealth. They enjoy greater human rights than they ever did in the past. And they've maintained their access to private health care and schooling, key factors in ensuring their high standard of living.

While many whites have migrated to other countries over the past two decades, if they've left Cape Town, then they've often had to give up quite a bit for the effort. In leaving this city, they've given up easy access to one of the most beautiful urban environments in the world. They now pay more for a comparable standard of living. They pay more for domestic help abroad, or cannot afford it all. And, let's be frank, they lose some of the privileges associated with their whiteness.

You see, when they move to majority-white countries like Australia, Canada, New Zealand, the UK, and the US, they can't leverage their whiteness as powerfully as they can here. As a minority tribe in Cape Town, they enjoy access to all kinds of informal considerations, networks, and opportunities which fall into their laps simply by virtue of their skin color and high-trust ethnic affiliation.

That's why, even though the government incentivizes black affirmative action—in hiring, management, and business ownership—whites have not been unduly affected by this. Far from it. They enjoy the lowest unemployment rate by race here. Don't listen to the troll who says, "There's no place for the white man in this country." Nonsense. According to almost any metric, white folks are doing just fine here.

Moreover, white South Africans' image has been rehabilitated internationally. No longer pariahs scorned by overseas whites for apartheid, they now form part of the global white elite.

Don't get me wrong. Whites may have it good in Cape Town, but they still face high levels of vulnerability and insecurity just by virtue of living here. Just like other Capetonians, they have been targets of vicious personal crimes.

So if they're fearful, and maybe want to leave the country because of it, it's not *necessarily* because of racial anxiety. It could be due to something more fundamental, concerning physical safety. Indeed, they put up with a level of insecurity that most white people abroad do not face, staying because they've made peace with this fact, and because...well... it's home.

There's certainly no other home out there for the smaller number of working-class whites who, for one reason or another, couldn't parlay their previous advantages into long-term prosperity. Living modestly in marginal suburbs, these poorer whites enjoy little of the prestige of their wealthier counterparts, and far fewer opportunities. For other Capetonians, these white folks are ambivalent figures, anomalies treated as objects of curiosity ("Wait, there are white people who aren't ridiculously wealthy in Cape Town? Tell me more!"), derision ("How on earth did these guys miss the apartheid gravy train? Idiots!"), or pity ("Shame, from the top of the heap to the bottom. They're screwed now.").

And though this group is often criticized as being racist, they actually live more racially integrated lives than their wealthier cousins. They didn't flee their suburbs, as middle-class whites did, when upwardly mobile coloureds and Africans started moving in. They stayed put because, for better or worse, it's home. (And because they probably couldn't afford to leave.)

Whatever the case, what would Cape Town be without the Afrikaner, English, Greek, Jewish, and Portuguese communities here? It's hard to imagine.

∿

For coloureds, the liberation dividend has been a mixed blessing. They have their political freedom, yes, but economically, working-class coloureds have stagnated post-'94. Because they had enjoyed job protections in the apartheid era vis-à-vis the African working class, they did not reap many economic benefits from that racist policy coming to an end. And this is one of the reasons why a number of working-class coloureds feel bitter about some of the changes that have occurred since. As a middle minority that was simultaneously oppressed and privileged, liberation was certain to bring some ironic side-effects.

Middle-class coloureds, though, have done much better. Having been frustrated by the "whites only" job reservation policies in the professional sectors, freedom meant finally being allowed to compete with whites on a more equitable footing. They consequently rose up the ranks, establishing themselves as key players in a number of white collar fields. They now enjoy good standards of living, travel abroad, lease fancy cars, and put their kids in expensive "former white" schools (the Holy Grail for many upwardly mobile coloured parents).

But, as we've seen, they can often feel frustrated by the social dynamics of the workplace where whites are better poised through their social networks to continue dominating the professions.

One thing that unites all coloureds is their increasing exposure to what seems like an epidemic of diabetes, obesity, and heart disease. Over the past twenty years, a worrying proportion of them have developed one or more of these conditions, leading to compromised health outcomes and early death. My wife's dad died at 64, a day before he was to go in for a second amputation of toes on his foot for diabetes. One of my best friends here, a chef at sea, had to be airlifted from a diamond rig off the coast of Namibia to get an emergency amputation which took most of his leg. He was still in his 40s. The stories are endless. So are the insulin jabs, trips to the public hospitals, mini-strokes followed by major ones, sore chests, and rounds of medication. (Some sufferers even "brag" about all the pills they have to take, as if it were a competition. Sitting together at family functions, they compare notes with a dark, ironic sense of humor.)

This is the curse for people who are too poor to buy fresh, wholesome foods, but rich enough to live near supermarkets selling cheap, sugary, salty, canned, concentrated, never-expiring franken-foods packaged by corporate behemoths and advertised as healthy. ("Enriched with Vitamin D. Low carb. Fat free." You know the drill.) Basically, their diet—viewed from a nutritional lens—looks a lot like that of working-class

Americans and Brits. Which is to say, shocking.

But so many of the foods that coloureds enjoy happen to be really tasty! When I was staying in Mitchell's Plain, I lived with a family that ran a *Gatsby* and chip roll shop from their house. I'd sometimes help out, selling these monster baguettes stuffed with oily *chips* (French fries), *polony* (bologna) slices, lettuce, and tomatoes. All slathered in mayo, salt, and spicy ketchup. Enough calories to feed a hospital. (The very place you end up after the fifth bite.) Couple these take-away meals with the lovely aromatic dishes prepared in their kitchens—full of fried chicken, roasted meats, gravy, grilled sausages, white rice, and potatoes—you've got the recipe for, unfortunately, hypertension, clogged arteries, and insulin resistance.

Their African neighbors across the tracks are starting to suffer some of these same urban lifestyle diseases. But the greatest health disaster that they have faced since liberation is the HIV/AIDS crisis which hit Africans disproportionately hard. Most, if not all, Capetonian Africans know someone who has died from AIDS-related complications, or someone who is living with HIV today, surviving because of life-saving antiretrovirals (ARVs). In years past, this emergency consumed the nation, but more recently appears to have stabilized as the government got its act together regarding treatment protocols and health care access. Today, the disease is no longer a death sentence. Far from it. It's rather another element of life that one tries to avoid (if they don't have it) or manage with daily medication (if they do).

And yet, since the townships remain the residential horizon for most coloureds and Africans, these areas have seen dramatic changes over the years. Residents upgraded their houses to make their lives more comfortable. They've built additions in their backyards to house rent-paying boarders or their own expanding families. And they've invested in their communities, participating in social uplift programs while trying to make their neighborhoods safer.

Indeed, when tourists come to Cape Town and embark on their obligatory township tours, they are rarely taken to the former coloured areas as they do not appear poor enough. The houses look modest, but often also cared for and cozy. Parts of the older African townships built before or during apartheid are also sometimes given a skip as they look relatively solid, not the hellholes that tourists expect. They don't conform to the "poverty porn" images that outsiders hope to see.

Yes, those who take township tours will get to watch gumboot dancers at some civic hall, see a sheep's head split open and grilled at the market, meet a shebeen queen and taste the local brew, ask the urban herbalist about her plants, and take some selfies with a "well-spoken" community organizer. But none of this reeks of the poverty they often still associate with "apartheid" and "Africa." So, oftentimes these tours end up focusing more on the severely distressed informal settlements on the edge of the townships which—

while certainly a product of an apartheid legacy and continued housing shortages—are not, strictly speaking, "townships." (They're shantytowns.)

The ironies of this aside, it is a credit to Capetonians that they have been successful at transforming many aspects of their former residential jails into thriving communities where families can be raised with a degree of hope for the future. These places continue to face their fair share of difficulties—like the ubiquity of crime, drug use, gangsterism, and unemployment—but as a people who survived one of the most repressive regimes of the 20th Century, Capetonians have shown themselves more than capable of surviving their freedom in the 21st as well.

∿∿

Last story, I promise. Some years back I worked for an online magazine showcasing all the cool cafes, restaurants, shops, events, and destinations in Cape Town. While there, I got to attend 5-star hotel openings, taste the brew at new cafes, review flamboyant drag shows, groove to funky jazz licks at the latest underground clubs, and size up the tasty tapas at new eateries. I was even tasked with writing about the opening of a small restaurant inside an S&M bondage shop, of all places. ("Waiter, I'll have a Greek salad and a pair of furry handcuffs, please.")

I also got to research other fun topics like the world of local soccer fandom, basically why Capetonians are more obsessed with overseas teams than their own. I looked into the influx of Eastern European girls to local strip clubs like Mavericks, Teasers, Arabesque, and Kinky's. And I investigated the healing techniques of urban *sangomas* (healers) whose windshield-wiper leaflets promise relief from money problems, love troubles, weak erections, and premature ejaculation. (Top *that*, Dr Oz!)

But the greatest part of this job was being able to work in offices right in the beating heart of the city. Long Street. From my office window, I could see and hear the bustle of one of the most diverse scenes in Cape Town. A procession of young and old, male and female, gay and straight, and every race, color, and faith. All sorts, just walking, shopping, chilling, squatting, touting, flirting, hawking, muttering, hollering, driving, hooting, car-guarding, and double-parking. An organic, multi-layered scene, vibrating on that edge between harmony and discord, symphony, and cacophony.

Long Street was edgy but safe (well, safe *enough*), with an invigorating ambience. And the streets paralleling and intersecting it expanded this vibey character, acting as spaces of openings, accessibility, possibility, unpredictability, and energy. They still do (see image 8).

In many ways, these downtown streets represent the best of what Cape Town can be: a city of connection. Connecting past, present, and future. Locals with visitors.

But it's a street whose verve and vitality could never be

simply planned—like one of the city's anodyne suburban malls—as it has emerged over centuries, through constant reinvention. Nevertheless, it is a space that must be nurtured and protected. Criminals and corpo rates want access to the pockets of those striding this street. Both must be managed and kept at a distance to allow Capetonians to connect on terms that are not determined by the fear of violence, or the threat of gentrification.

Compare these streets to the rest of the city where most spaces remain highly exclusionary. Former African townships have a similar demographic profile to the one they did during apartheid. Same with the former coloured townships. Same with the wealthier former white areas.

It's only in the middle-class areas that professional families of every background have been able to accommodate themselves to a more diverse reality. But because middle-class families tend not to base their friendships on neighborly proximity, but rather on religious, school, or work affiliations, these mixed suburbs do not hold much promise of becoming spaces where we might find new patterns of multi-racial engagement.

That certainly describes my family's current living situation in Century City, a new-build area with houses, apartments, office blocks, and a huge shopping mall. Post-dating apartheid, the area hosts a motley mix of Indians from Durban, Africans from Joburg, local middle-class coloureds, young white couples, overseas Chinese, European transplants, and Middle Eastern entrepreneurs. It's a pleasantly mixed area.

But the one thing it is not is a community. We all live separate lives, rarely engaging each other beyond polite greetings. No one feels any sense of obligation to the other. In fact, if anything, residents' obligations remain with the people they left behind to live in Century City, like family and friends in the townships. Marj goes to Kensington almost every day to see her sisters. It's the same for many of our neighbors who spend their free time in the townships and remit money to family members in the rural areas or abroad.

The place where new forms of multi-racial engagement is more likely to happen, though, is at middle-class schools which have become melting pots of the city. They offer children of every background the chance to learn, play, and compete together, and hopefully build bonds of trust that gradually diminish race as a factor in their future prospects. It also creates ties of affection between the parents who find common ground with each other through shared desires for their children. Indeed, virtually all of the new friends that Marj and I have made over the past few years have been through our daughter's school as we've grown closer to her classmates' parents. Even though we come from wildly different backgrounds, our kids are able to connect us.

Similar changes are happening in the workplace, especially the professions where the educated middle class congregate, but there are limits, as we've discussed above. Work places still reproduce racial and gender divisions, especially at the top end of business structures.

Capetonians also mingle in recreational spaces and sporting venues, especially those from a similar class background. And it is in these more casual environments —where meat and alcohol are shared—that low-stakes fraternization can gently erode the barriers that have traditionally divided this city.

But, is this it? Is this interracial "mingling" at school, work, bars, and stadiums the best that Capetonians can expect if they live in the suburbs or townships?

Considering that this remains one of the most unequal cities in the world: yes, probably, for the time being.

∿∿

Cape Town is a city that feels like it is always on the cusp of arriving but never quite getting there. Like an interminable project, or an "emerging economy" that just keeps emerging, but never fully developing.

A city in permanent limbo. Two steps forward, one-and-a-half steps back. (With a side-to-side shimmy.)

IN/BETWEEN AFRICA

in closing, an opening

For Capetonians, the images conjured by the name *Africa* overlap only slightly with those conjured by *Cape Town*. A fact which is an indictment to some, proof of a pathological fixation on old hierarchies. Colonized minds insisting on keeping things *imperial* in a *post*-imperial world.

Yet to others this is a relief, a suggestion that the Peninsula sticking itself far out into the ocean is distinct from the continent to which it seems so tenuously attached.

Indeed, no other metro in Africa creates such a tension between a city's identity and that of its embracing continent, between the expectations we have of it and what it actually gives.

On the one hand, it is a natural wonder, with no end to its delights. On the other, it is a natural disaster where lives are casually snuffed out in paroxysms of violence. A warm, embracing Mother City for some, a cold and indifferent step-mother for others.

Cape Town is that space between Africa the *real* and Africa the *imagined*. A place in/between Africa.

∿∿

In this book, I've asked that you not only embrace the beauty of this city, but to also—while in that embrace—run your fingers along its scars, its burns, its wounds.

Hold it as you would a lover. Not as a body that is perfect, flawless. But a shape with hidden depths, shadowed bruises, signs of past traumas.

A body whose form entices you visually and—once you accept this Cape as it is, in its bewildering complexity—satisfies you emotionally.

This means reckoning with the awkward fact that Cape Town fits into almost none of the categories we employ when thinking about Africa. About black, white, east, west, developed, underdeveloped, first and third worlds. Concepts that otherwise help us navigate this confounding and captivating continent.

So I've invited you to explore this ambiguous, in-terstitial, hybrid, creole, mixed, in-between city that is unlike any other in Africa and, perhaps, the world. My humble hope is that this exploration has enlivened your own understanding of the place and opened up new questions as you engage with it and its people.

Of course, my take is provisional, fragmented, incomplete. This city is too multifaceted to take it all in at once. So, here I've used the metaphor of in-betweenness to explore and illuminate the histories, cultures, politics, and prospects of this city. I've done so not because the city actually *is* in-between anything, but because it is how locals themselves understand this city and their experiences in it. It's also one of the first impressions that visitors have, a sense of familiarity with other places, and yet difference.

This means that my approach reveals as much about me/us as it does the city. We're all co-conspirators in shaping a subjective truth about Cape Town.

The virtue of this approach is that it allows us to highlight and take joy in the uniqueness of this metropolis. It's such a spectacular city! We shouldn't lose sight of that even as the picture gets murky. But the downside is that we can fall into the trap of moralizing it as either "better than" some imaginary polar concept or "less than" it (especially the concept of *Africa*). We struggle to just embrace Cape Town as it is, in all of its staggering ambiguity, tempted to compare it to or rank it against other places.

For me, understanding Cape Town the city has helped me better understand Africa the continent. It has enlarged my sense of it. Rather than dismissing the city as too different, I see it as contributing to the cornucopia of cultures that constitute Africa. This is because, by the time I first visited Cape Town, I had already spent three years meandering through 14 other African countries. And while there were many similarities across these places, there wasn't sameness. What struck me most was how diverse all of the countries were. As the oldest continent in the world, the birthplace of humankind, where cultures, languages, styles, and traditions have been evolving longer than anywhere else, this should be expected.

Yet, in most of our minds, including Capetonians', *Africa* is reduced to static images of disease, poverty, corruption, war, nature, animals, and mono-racial blackness. With such narrow stereotypes shaping perceptions, it is no wonder that Cape Town is often seen as being "outside" the African experience. But our reliance on such myopic images robs us of the generative processes involved in broadening our perspective, and grappling with the uncertainty and anxiety we often feel about a city that appears to playfully flit between multiple, contradictory ideals.

Perhaps my interest in using in-betweenness as a lens to understand this city also comes from the fact that I'm now middle aged (noooo!), that I've lived overseas for as many years as I've lived in the land of my birth, that I've moved from outsider status in Cape Town to insider, or that I've grown wary of any politics that seeks to marginalize non-normative peoples, places, cultures, or histories. I've come to feel more at home in in-between spaces and thinking about their potential in acting as bridges for commonality rather than chasms of difference.

Because of that, I am proud to call Cape Town my adopted home, and I'm thrilled to have been able to share some of my thoughts about it with you. We can remember it as our shared adventure in ambivalence.

Thanks!

See you around. *Hamba kahle. Totsiens.*

GLOSSARY & ACRONYMS

GLOSSARY

Baas	boss (Afrikaans)
Bantu	literally "people" (Bantu languages) referring here to South African speakers of Bantu languages
Bantustan	territories established by the apartheid government as "homelands" for African residents; proposed as "independent countries," but never recognized as such outside Pretoria
Bastards	derogatory term for children born out of wedlock (English), but also referring non-derogatorily to a particular coloured ethnic group, the Basters (Afrikaans) of Namibia
Bioscope	cinema (South African English, dated)
Bobotie	spiced minced meat baked with an egg-based topping (Afrikaans, of Javanese origin)
Boesmans	Bushmen (Afrikaans), most often used as a slur
Boetie	brother (Afrikaans, informal)
Braai	grilled/grilling meat (Afrikaans), a key social bonding ritual for most South Africans
Bredie	slow-cooked stew (Afrikaans)
Bruinmense	brown people (Afrikaans), an older term to refer to coloured people
Camissa	Cape Town (Khoi), promoted by some

	Khoisan revivalists as an alternative word for "coloured"
Chips	French fries (British/SA English)
Cordons sanitaires	barriers to prevent the spread of disease, or movement of people (French)
Dagga	marijuana (Afrikaans, from Khoi language)
Gam	from Ham, son of Noah whose lineage is cursed into perpetual bondage (Cape Afrikaans), slang slur to mean "low-class" coloured
Gatsby	long baguette filled with meat, lettuce, tomato slices, mayo and other items (derived from the 1974 film adaptation of *The Great Gatsby* by F. Scott Fitzgerald, in reference to the "great" size of the sandwich), popular as a shareable working-class food
Ghoema	portable, barrel-shaped drum (Bantu, from ngoma) that produces the upbeat syncopated rhythms of ghoema music, as expressed in the music of the Minstrel Carnival
Gqom	minimalist form of house music (Zulu), using jerky, repetitive beat patterns
Hamba kahle	go well (Xhosa), good bye
Hotstix	Sipho "Hotstix" Mabuse, legendary South African musician
Hottentots	derogatory term referring to the Khoisan (Dutch) by Dutch and English settlers at the Cape
Jolling	partying (Afrikaans)

Kaapenaars   Capetonians (Afrikaans)

Kaapse Klopse   literally "Cape clubs" (Afrikaans),
                   referring to the annual Cape Minstrel
                   Coon Carnival

Kaapse taal   Cape language (Afrikaans), referring to
                   the unique form of Afrikaans spoken by
                   Cape Town coloureds, which mixes
                   Afrikaans, older Dutch variations, English
                   and Indonesian

Kaffirs   literally "unbelievers" (Arabic), used as
                   a dehumanizing racial epithet to refer to
                   Africans, especially in the colonial and
                   apartheid eras; its use today is often
                   considered a human rights violation;
                   when discussed analytically, it is usually
                   referred to as "the K-word" (similar to
                   the N-word in US English)

Khoi   literally "people" (Nama), the indigenous
                   hunters and herders of the Cape; this is
                   a contested term

Khoisan   collective designation for the Khoi
                   (hunters and herders) and San (hunter-
                   gatherers) of the Cape and beyond; this
                   is a contested term

Kleurlings   coloureds (Afrikaans)

Koeksisters   fried dough bathed in honey or syrup
                   (Afrikaans)

Labarang   Eid al-fitr (Indonesian, from the word
                   "Ramadan"; now Cape Afrikaans)

Lobola   bride price (Zulu), traditionally paid in
                   cattle but now also with cash and other
                   types of gifts

Mandrax	Methaqualone (known in the US as Quaaludes), a sedative and hypnotic medication
Meisie	girl (Afrikaans), often historically used to mean "maid"
Mielie	maize cob (South African English)
Moer hom	hit him hard (Afrikaans), kick his ass
Moffie	derogatory term for effeminate homo-sexual man (Afrikaans, likely derived from hermaphrodite); in the Cape Minstrel Carnival, it refers to a troupe's drag queen mascot
Mos	an intensifier word (Cape Afrikaans)
Nagtroupe	night troupes (Afrikaans), referring to the Malay Choir night marches
Polony	bologna (Afrikaans), processed meat
Potjie	small pot (Afrikaans), here referring to a cast-iron pot used to cook a layered mix of food over fire
San	literally "foragers" (Khoi), indigenous hunter-gatherer groups in the Cape and across Southern Africa; this is a contested term
Sangoma	traditional healers (Zulu), who use a combination of herbal, ritual, and spiritual mechanisms to address personal and social ills
Shebeen	illicit tavern (Irish), often run by women
Sisi	sister (Xhosa, from Afrikaans)
Sjambok	rawhide whip (Afrikaans), and symbol of oppression
Stoep	porched-in veranda (Afrikaans)

Suikerhuisie	literally sugar house (Afrikaans), brothel
Swart gevaar	black fear (Afrikaans), a fear-mongering tactic that has been used to politically mobilize whites and coloureds against African political groups
Tafel	table (Afrikaans), here referring to the tables of refreshment set up for minstrels at various township homes as they entertain their communities
Tik	crystal meth (Afrikaans)
Totsiens	until we meet again (Afrikaans), goodbye
Toyi-toyi	protest dancing (Shona), which includes stomping, high-stepping and side-to-side movements in rhythm with singing and chanting
Tweede Nuwe Jaar	January 2nd (Afrikaans), the day that the Cape Minstrel Carnival marches the downtown route
Ulwaluko	circumcision and initiation rite (Xhosa) of teenage Xhosa males into manhood
Volk	a people or cultural group (Afrikaans)
Voorlooper	literally front walker (Afrikaans), referring to a Minstrel Carnival troupe's lead marcher who is usually an entertaining dancer for the crowds
Wamkelekile	welcome (Xhosa)
Welkom	welcome (Afrikaans)
Wors	sausage (Afrikaans)

ACRONYMS

ACDP	African Christian Democratic Party
AIDS	Acquired Immune Deficiency Syndrome
ANC	African National Congress
ARV	antiretroviral medication
BPNCC	Black People's National Crisis Committee
COPE	Congress of the People
DA	Democratic Alliance
EFF	Economic Freedom Fighters
FF+	Freedom Front Plus
HIV	Human Immunodeficiency Virus
ID	Independent Democrats
IFP	Inkatha Freedom Party
MP	Member of Parliament
NP	National Party
PAC	Pan Africanist Congress
PAGAD	People Against Gangsterism and Drugs
SA	South Africa
SACP	South African Communist Party
UCT	University of Cape Town
UDF	United Democratic Front
UK	United Kingdom
US	United States
UWC	University of the Western Cape
UZ	University of Zimbabwe

PHOTO DESCRIPTIONS & CREDITS

See 8-page photo insert

1. **Iconic Cape Town**
   Photo by © Kierran Allen, 2015
   (Reprinted with permission from iStock)

2. **Residential Inequality**
   Photo by © fivepointsix, 2018
   (Reprinted with permission from iStock)

3. **District Six Life and its Destruction**
   Top: Girls Skipping Rope on Upper Ashley Street
   by © Cloete Breytenbach, 1960
   (Reprinted with permission from Leon Breytenbach)
   Bottom: Demolition of a block in Bloemhof Flats
   by © Jimi Matthews, early 1980s
   *(Reprinted with permission from Jimi Matthews and
   the District Six Museum)*

4. **Dockside Nightlife @ The Catacombs**
   Photos by Billy Monk, 1967
   (Reprinted with permission from © Craig Cameron-Mackintosh)

5. **Minstrel in the Cape Town Minstrel Carnival**
   Photo by © Henry Trotter, 2001

6. **The Extended Bingham Family**
   Photo by © Henry Trotter, 2001

7. **Rhodes Must Fall Student Protests at UCT**
   Photo by © David Harrison, 2015
   (Reprinted with permission from David Harrison)

8. **Urban Art and Long Street**
   Photos by © Henry Trotter, 2018
   Mural artists:
   Brian Rolfe (Nelson Mandela and Desmond Tutu)
   Garth Wareley (Winnie Madikizela-Mandela)

FURTHER READING & INFO

While there remains much to be written about Cape Town's history, culture, and politics, a lot of practical information —regarding the events, stats, quotes, and personalities mentioned in this book—can be found online. Just google them. In most cases, you'll find corroborating (or conflicting) info on the issues raised here.

But if you're like me, you'll also want to get your hands on a good old-fashioned book and engage this world more deeply. Here are a few I can recommend that shed more light on Cape Town, and its place in South Africa, Africa and the world.

ON HISTORY

Adhikari, Mohamed. *The Anatomy of a South African Genocide: The Extermination of the Cape San Peoples* (2011).

Bickford-Smith, Vivian, Elizabeth van Heyningen & Nigel Worden. *Cape Town in the Twentieth Century: An Illustrated Social History* (1999).

Bickford-Smith, Vivian & Elizabeth van Heyningen. *The Waterfront* (1994).

Brodie, Nechama. *The Cape Town Book: A Guide to the City's History, People and Places* (2015).

Clark, Nancy & William Worger. *South Africa: The Rise and Fall of Apartheid* (2011).

Crais, Clifton & Pamela Scully. *Sara Baartman and the Hottentot Venus: A Ghost Story and a Biography* (2008).

Elphick, Richard & Hermann Giliomee (Eds). *The Shaping of South African Society, 1652–1840*, 2nd ed. (1988).

Giliomee, Herman. *The Afrikaners: Biography of a People* (2010).

La Guma, Alex. *A Walk in the Night* (1962).

Marx, Anthony. *Making Race and Nation: A Comparison of the United States, South Africa, and Brazil* (1998).

McKinnon, June. *A Tapestry of Lives: Cape Women of the 17th Century* (2004).

Nasson, Bill. *The War for South Africa: The Anglo-Boer War 1899–1902* (2011).

Phillips, Howard. *Plague, Pox and Pandemics: A Jacana Pocket History of Epidemics in South Africa* (2012).

Shell, Robert. *Children of Bondage: A Social History of the Slave Society at the Cape of Good Hope, 1652–1838* (1994).

Smith, Charlene. *Robben Island* (2013).

van der Ross, Richard. *Up from Slavery: Slaves at the Cape: Their Origins, Treatment and Contribution* (2005).

van Onselen, Charles. *The Fox and the Flies: The World of Joseph Silver, Racketeer and Psychopath* (2007).

Vinson, Robert Trent. *The Americans Are Coming!: Dreams of African American Liberation in Segregationist South Africa* (2012).

Ward, Kerry. *Networks of Empire: Forced Migration in the Dutch East India Company* (2008).

Worden, Nigel. *The Making of Modern South Africa: Conquest, Apartheid, Democracy*, 5th Ed (2012).

Worden, Nigel, Elizabeth van Heyningen & Vivian Bickford-Smith. *Cape Town—The Making of a City: An Illustrated Social History* (1998).

*ALSO VISIT THE SOUTH AFRICAN MUSEUM, THE CHAVONNES

BATTERY MUSEUM, THE CASTLE OF GOOD HOPE, THE SLAVE LODGE, BERTRAM HOUSE, THE GROOT CONSTANTIA MANOR HOUSE, THE KOOPMANS-DE WET HOUSE, THE NAVAL MUSEUM, RUST EN VREUGD, THE HOLOCAUST CENTRE, THE HEART OF CAPE TOWN MUSEUM, AND THE ROBBEN ISLAND MUSEUM.

ON POLITICS

Bundy, Colin. *Short-Changed? South Africa Since Apartheid* (2014).

Butler, Anthony. *The Idea of the ANC* (2013).

Carlin, John. *Playing the Enemy: Nelson Mandela and the Game That Made a Nation* (2009).

Mandela, Nelson. *Long Walk to Freedom* (1994).

Pauw, Jacques. *The President's Keepers: Those Keeping Zuma in Power and out of Prison* (2017).

Sparks, Allister. *Tomorrow Is Another Country: The Inside Story of South Africa's Road to Change* (1996).

Tutu, Desmond. *No Future Without Forgiveness* (2000).

*ALSO VISIT PARLIAMENT TO ATTEND A SESSION.

ON CULTURE

Biko, Steve. *I Write What I Like* (1978).

Field, Sean, Renate Meyer & Felicity Swanson (Eds). *Imagining the City: Memories and Cultures in Cape Town* (2007).

Gaulier, Armelle & Denis-Constant Martin. *Cape Town Harmonies: Memory, Humour and Resilience* (2017).

Hugill, Stan. *Sailortown* (1967).

Mafeje, Archie & Monica Wilson. *Langa: A Study of Social Groups in an African Township* (1963).

Mason, John Edward. *One Love, Ghoema Beat: Inside the Cape Town Carnival* (2010).

Martin, Denis-Constant. *Sounding the Cape: Music, Identity and Politics in South Africa* (2013).

Martin, Denis-Constant. *Coon Carnival: New Year in Cape Town, Past and Present* (1999).

Ramphele, Mamphela. *A Bed Called Home: Life in the Migrant Labour Hostels of Cape Town* (1993).

Trotter, Henry. *Sugar Girls & Seamen: A Journey into the World of Dockside Prostitution in South Africa* (2008).

Worden, Nigel (Ed.). *Cape Town Between East and West: Social Identities in a Dutch Colonial Town* (2012).

*ALSO VISIT THE SA MARITIME CENTRE, JEWISH MUSEUM, THE NATIONAL GALLERY, THE SPRINGBOK EXPERIENCE, THE IRMA STERN MUSEUM, THE DIAMOND MUSEUM, THE ZEITZ MUSEUM OF CONTEMPORARY ART AFRICA.

ON COLOURED IDENTITY

Adhikari, Mohamed. *Burdened By Race: Coloured Identities in Southern Africa* (2009).

Adhikari, Mohamed. *Not White Enough, Not Black Enough: Racial Identity in the South African Coloured Community* (2005).

Erasmus, Zimitri (Ed). *Coloured by History, Shaped by Place: New Perspectives on Coloured Identities in Cape Town* (2001).

Goldin, Ian. *Making Race: The Politics and Economics of Coloured Identity in South Africa* (1987).

James, Wilmot, Daria Caliguire & Kerry Cullinan (Eds). *Now That We Are Free: Coloured Communities in a Democratic South Africa* (1996).

Jung, Courtney. *Then I Was Black: South African Political Identities in Transition* (2000).

Lewis, Gavin. *Between the Wire and the Wall: A History*

of South African 'Coloured' Politics (1987).

Pickel, Birgit. *Coloured Ethnicity and Identity: A Case Study in the former coloured areas in the Western Cape / South Africa* (1997).

*ALSO VISIT THE BO-KAAP MUSEUM.

ON FORCED REMOVALS

Breytenbach, Cloete. *The Spirit of District Six* (1997).

Ebrahim, Noor. *Noor's Story: My Life in District Six* (1999).

Field, Sean (Ed). *Lost Communities, Living Memories: Remembering Forced Removals in Cape Town* (2001).

Fortune, Linda. *The House in Tyne Street: Childhood Memories of District Six* (1996).

Jeppie, Shamil & Crain Soudien (Eds). *The Struggle for District Six: Past and Present* (1990).

Kube, Gloria & Ruby Hill. *Living in Loader Street* (1996).

Ngcelwane, Nomvuyo. *Sala Kahle, District Six* (1998).

Rassool, Yousuf. *District Six—Lest We Forget: Recapturing Subjugated Cultural Histories of Cape Town, 1897–1956* (2000).

Rive, Richard. *Buckingham Palace: District Six* (1986).

Thomas, Gladys. *Avalon Court: Vignettes of Life of the 'Coloured' People on the Cape Flats of Cape Town* (1992).

Trotter, Henry. *Removals and Remembrance: Commemorating Community in Coloured Cape Town* (2002).

Western, John. *Outcast Cape Town* (1981).

*AND VISIT THE DISTRICT SIX MUSEUM.

ON GANGSTERISM IN CAPE TOWN

Jensen, Steffen. *Gangs, Politics and Dignity in Cape Town* (2008).

Lindegaard, Marie Rosenkrantz. *Surviving Gangs, Violence and Racism in Cape Town: Ghetto Chameleons* (2017).

Pinnock, Don. *Gang Town* (2016).

Steinberg, Jonny. *The Number: One Man's Search for Identity in the Cape Underworld and Prison Gangs* (2005).

ON CONTEMPORARY SOCIETY

Christie, Sean. *Under Nelson Mandela Boulevard: Life Among the Stowaways* (2016).

Coetzee, J.M. *Disgrace: A Novel* (2000).

Gish, Steven. *Amy Biehl's Last Home: A Bright Life, a Tragic Death, and a Journey of Reconciliation in South Africa* (2018).

Habib, Adam. *Rebels and Rage: Reflections on #FeesMustFall* (2019).

Nicol, Mike. *Sea-Mountain, Fire City: Living in Cape Town* (2001).

Nyamnjoh, Francis. *#RhodesMustFall: Nibbling at Resilient Colonialism in South Africa* (2016).

Omotoso, Yewande. *The Woman Next Door: A Novel* (2017).

Otter, Steven. *Khayelitsha: uMlungu in a Township* (2007).

Salo, Elaine. *Respectable Mothers, Tough Men and Good Daughters: Producing Persons in Manenberg Township South Africa* (2018).

Southall, Roger. *The New Black Middle Class in South Africa* (2016).

Watson, Stephen (Ed). *Cape Town—A City Imagined* (2012).

ON COLOURED NOMENCLATURE

Citations for the list of names given to coloureds over time (p.77):

Cape people, half-castes, and *white Kaffirs,* ooo Sarah Gertrude Millin, *The South Africans* (1934).

God's stepchildren, see Millin, *God's Stepchildren* (1924).

Bastards, see Millin, *King of the Bastards* (1949), though Bastards also refers to an ethnic group centered in Rehoboth, Namibia.

Hottentots, Eurafricans, and *half-breeds,* see W.M. MacMillan, *The Cape Colour Question* (1927).

racial hybrids, middle minority, and *buffer group,* see F. James Davis, *Who Is Black?: One Nation's Definition* (1991).

mixed-bloods and *marginal men,* see John William Mann, *The Problem of the Marginal Personality: A Psychological Study of a Coloured Group* (1957).

marginal men, see also H.F. Dickie-Clark, *The Marginal Situation: A Sociological Study of a Coloured Group* (1966).

in-betweeners, see E.J. Doman, "The In-Betweeners: A Look at the Coloured People of South Africa," *in Optima* (1975).

brown Afrikaners, see Peter Marais, "Too Long in the Twilight," in Wilmot James, et al., eds., *Now That We are Free: Coloured Communities in a Democratic South Africa* (1996).

middle children, see Rayda Jacobs, *The Middle Children* (1994).

twilight people, see David Houze, *Twilight People: One Man's Journey to Find His Roots* (2006).

blacks, see wide variety of scholars and politicos (such

as Nelson Mandela and Steve Biko)

so-called coloureds, (often in quotation marks), see
writings by the Non-European Unity Movement
(NEUM), as discussed by Mohamed Adkhikari,
"Fiercely Non-Racial? Discourses and Politics of Race
in the Non-European Unity Movement, 1943–70," in
Journal of Southern African Studies 31/2 (2005).

people of mixed race, the most common short-hand for
describing coloured people (especially informally)

Camissa, a Khoi term referring to Cape Town and
promoted as an alternative to "coloured," see
camissapeople.wordpress.com

kleurlings (coloureds) and *bruinmense* (brown people)
are commonly used Afrikaans terms, *Boesmans*
(Bushmen) and *gam* (meaning "low-class" coloureds,
in a reference to Ham, son of Noah, whose lineage
is cursed into perennial servitude) are Afrikaans slurs,
sometimes used by coloureds critiquing or mocking
each other.

ACKNOWLEDGEMENTS

This book has been more than twenty years in the making. Along the way I have amassed major personal, emotional and intellectual debts with countless people. Colleagues who have nurtured and challenged me. Friends who have strengthened and encouraged me. Family members who have loved and supported me. To them, I express my gratitude.

The list of those who have shaped and enhanced my life in Cape Town—and therefore how I understand it—is vast. Some of them have done so unwittingly, or in small ways, and others in profound and sustained ways. Some have done so in Cape Town, some from afar. I want to acknowledge them all. This is the kind of book where it is right to do so.

To the *educators, academics, and mentors* who have given so generously to me, thank you: Mohamed Adhikari, Edward Antonio, Vivian Bickford-Smith, Ann Biersteker, Ken Brown, Kennedy Chinyowa, Randy Cox, Susan Dewey, Uma Duphelia-Mesthrie, Bill Fitzhenry, John Keefe, Ben Kiernan, Mike Mahoney, Mbongeni Malaba, Pedzisai Mashiri, John Mason, Peter Merrington, Rob Morrell, Bill Nasson, John Oriji, Rob Pattman, Gordon Pirie, Ciraj Rassool, Carina Ray, Jeremy Rich, Christopher Saunders, Debora Schwartz, Jim Scott, Gaddis Smith, Lance van Sittert, Dorothy Woodson, Eric Worby, Nigel Worden, and Keith Wrightson. With special thanks to Nancy Clark, Bob Harms, Sandra Sanneh, and Bill Worger.

To *colleagues* who have opened their hearts to me while expanding my mind during my time in Cape Town,

I thank you: Patricia Arinto, Girish Kumar Beeharry, Tess Cartmill, Alan Cliff, Raj Dhanarajan, Michael Glover, Eve Gray, Maria Ng Lee Hoon, Wilmot James, Catherine Kell, Annalie Lotriet, Kingo Mchombu, Sanjaya Mishra, Fred Mulder, Jacques Mushaandja, Olugbade Oladokun, Lighton Phiri, Vinand Prayag, Marlise Richter, Meenu Sharma, Ramesh Sharma, Matthew Smith, Atul Thakur, Angelina Totolo, François van Schalkwyk, Sukaina Walji, Nicole Withers, Stavros Xanthopoylos, Wilson Yule, and Batbold Zagdragchaa. With special thanks to Glenda Cox, Laura Czerniewicz, Cheryl Hodgkinson-Williams, Thomas King, and Michelle Willmers.

For those who helped me better understand the impact of *forced removals* on Cape Town society: Annie Bam, Jean Blanckenberg, Menisha Collins, Noor Ebrahim, Hajira Esau, Linda Fortune, Marilyn and Michael Hartzenberg, Margaux Jordan, Valmont Layne, Nazeem Lowe, Ragmat Mallick, Yasmin Mohamed, Thulani Nxumalo, Alan Roberts, Willie Sales, Joey Schaffers, Ben Solomons, Norma Solomons, John Western, and Jenny Wilson. With special thanks to Mymoena Emjedi, Eileen Nomdo, and the more than one hundred removees who shared their life stories with me across the Cape peninsula.

Thanks also to those who have helped me learn more about *global maritime reality* and *Cape Town's port culture*: Chris Adams, Yusuf Agherdien, Laurel Andrews, Gerard and Sheila Assam, Edward Bremner, Randall Charters, Deanna Collins, Paul Daniels, John Davids, Clyde Davidson, Ibrahim Domingo, Peter du Toit, Mike Fowkes, Bertram Fuscher, Patti Grange, Patricia Hosie, George House, Terry Hutson, Jonathan Hyslop, Brian Ingpen, Yusuf Ismail, Fred Jacobs, Samuel and Sarah Kim, Ivo Knobloch, Harold

Martin, Norman Meiring, Joewa Meyer, Keith Meyer, Melvin Mitchell, Abduragiem Mohamed, Tshego Mpye, Musa Msweli, Patrick O'Connell, Brian Omar, Paddy Percival, Brian Pettit, Charles Reid, Rion Ribeiro, Shaun Ruggunan, Ed Snyders, Inga Stanbridge, Jo Stanley, Peter Stowe, and Michael Wollenschlaeger. With special thanks to Vincent Kolbe, Eric and Marilyn Sobremonte, the *Reederei F. Laeisz* and *P&O Nedloyd* shipping lines (which allowed me to sail for two months on their container ships from Los Angeles to Cape Town in 2003), and the 200-plus other sailors, sugar girls, cabbies, and dockside nightclub owners who shared their stories with me.

To the amazing *scholars* and *writers* who shared an openness and desire to "undress" South African cities with me, I thank you for your generosity of spirit. In addition to some of the people already listed here, thank you to: (*Re Cape Town*) Andrew Brown, Armien Cassiem, Sean Christie, Andy Davis, Charl Fourie, Gino Fransman, Jade Gibson, Iain Harris, Ashraf Jamal, Julian Jonker, Yazeed Kamaldien, Craig Lewis, Sarah Lotz, Brent Meersman, Alexander Santillanes, and Janine Stephen; (*Re Durban*) Peter Bendheim, Sheetal Bhoola, Ashwin Desai, Tessa Diphoorn, Emma Durden, Thomas Blom Hansen, Crispin Hemson, Marlijn Knol, Molly Margaretten, Niall McNulty, Biniam Misgun, Zayn Nabbi, Kathryn Olsen, Thorin Roberts, Glen Thompson, and Goolam Vahed; (*Re Johannesburg*) Adam Ashforth, Utando Baduza, Heather Brookes, Marc Fletcher, Maria Frahm-Arp, Vincent Hoffman, Marcel Korth, Detlev Krige, Christo Lombaard, Dalitso Materechera, Kgebetli Moele, Dunbar Moodie, Samson Mulugeta, Ndumiso Ngcobo, Yoon Jung Park, Graeme Reid, Jonny Steinberg, and Caroline Suzman.

To the *Yalies* who made my intellectual journey from the States to Africa so enjoyable, Omolade Adunbi, Aisha Baastians, Justin Beckham, Martin Benjamin, Matt Bloom, Jerel Bryant, Ming-Qi Chu, Ben Conniff, Michelle de Saram, Judd Devermont, Martina Forgwe, Joseph Hill, Myra Jones-Taylor, Ranin Kazemi, Leah Khaghani, Matt Kustenbauder, Larissa Leclair, Lora LeMosy, Roger Levine, Cindy Lunsford, Thomas McDow, Manuella Meyer, Martin Nesvig, Shanti Parikh, Brian Peterson, Charles Riley, Theresa Runstedtler, Kwesi Sansculotte-Greenidge, Laura Seay, Charles and Sylvia Traeger, Lucia Trimbur, Charlotte Walker-Said, Erica Williams, and Michael Yarbrough. With special thanks to Ben Madley.

For my *comrades* and *friends* who have, at some point in my life, nurtured me, inspired me, pushed me, and sustained me, I salute you: Seeham Adams, Michelle Alfreds, Anwar Allie, Hazel Allies, Aubrey Arendse, Sindre Bangstad, Chris Beyers, Parmy Boual, Cezanne Britain-Renecke, Willem Burger, Ali Callaghan, Craig Cameron-Mackintosh, Margaret Chisholm, Rupert Chowins, Barry Cleveland, Abby Collins, Peter Cole, Chip Colwell, David Cordoso, Patricia Drummond-Decker, Steve Dunkle, Michael Eastman, Grace Edinger, Eve Fairbanks, Paul Faure, Tyler Fleming, Gavin Furlonger, Marcia Geschenk, Mona Hakimi, Paida Hakutangwi, David Harrison, Ross Harvey, Jeanne Hefez, Michelle Heswick, Iain Horner, Peter Hugo, Bridget Impey, Francesca Inglese, Gary Johnson, Vivien Jones, Randolf Jorberg, Karabo Kgoleng, Jenny Kline, Lizelle Kruger, Dorie and Hal Larson, Christopher Lee, Igshaan Lewis, Emily Leys, Kim Lisagor, Edwin Lombard, Noelene Mahabeer, Shivani Mansingh, Nondwe Maqubela, Steven Markovitz, Graham Martin,

Russell Martin, Sarah Mathis, Shanaaz and Christian Matuz, Mandisa Mbali, Kiyoko Kimura Morgan, Thato Mogotsi, Mike and Steve Morgenfeld, Anna Müller, Christopher Murray, Yasin Nadal, Cnooont Nemuramba, Ambre Nicolson, Lovelyn Nwadeyi, Erika Paterson, Elizabeth Perrill, Jervis Pennington, Per-Anders Pettersson, Ashlene Pingelly, Donwald Pressly, Rubin Renecke, Amelia Romano, Kathryn Sapnas, Roderick Sauls, Juergen Sauter, Brian Schoch, Susan Segar, Khadija Sharife, Natalie Simon, Meghna Singh, Andrea Stallbom, Grace Taylor, Angie Velasquez Thornton, Amritha Vaz, Mishkah and Sohail Wahab, Ben Williams, Quentin Williams, Trevor Wilkins, and Marc Zandhuis. With special thanks to Bradley Fisher, Henry Kwan, Munashe Mashiri, Nick Shuit, and Ayanda, Trudy, and Tunika Mhlanga.

To *family friends* who enrich our lives: Yolanda Abrahams, Gloria Arendse, Melanie Bond, Yolanda Cupido, Charne Green, Vernon Rodrigues, Geraldine Simons, Laatiefa Smith, and Michael Weeder. As well as Dwaine, Felicia, and Tania Benjamin; Don and Irene Bright; Jean, Kathy, Sean, and Tayla Cerf; Muriel Guineas and family; Dellsha and Stan Jacobs; David LeGrange and family; Alex, Andre, Samantha, and Tayla Martin; Gertrude Murray and family; Caleb, Callum, Janine, Kayo, and Paul Nathan; Gareth Brown, Ethan, and Wendy Nathan; Darlene and Ray Patrick; Chadwin, Clerish, and Elizabeth Piet; Natalie, Emma and Christian Petersen; and Wendy and Alfred Timotheus.

To *my wife's family*, thank you for welcoming me into the clan and being such a source of continuous joy: Beverly and Clem Abrahams; Roy Abrahams; Auriel, Jackson, Jerenique, Lizette, Rovaro, and Sybil Bayard; Claudia,

Donovan, Enreco, Ethan, Gavin, Lynn, Reuben, Russell, and Wendy Bingham; Andre, Lyle, Lynn, and Shireen Cox; Colleen and Eddie Fortuin; Melvyn, Melvyn Jr., Sherwin, Shirley, and Tracy Fortune; Baden Gillion and Emma Wells; Junaide Gillion and Lorenzo Peters; Damien, Deidre, and Mark Jurias. With special thanks to Marjorie's mother, Kathleen, who is greatly missed.

I must also acknowledge the *generous financial support* that has allowed me to spend so much time in South Africa as an academic. My deepest thanks to: Rotary International for a Rotary Ambassadorial Scholarship; Yale University (the Center for African Studies and the Department of History), especially the MacMillan Center for International Studies and the Program in Agrarian Studies; Yale's Fox Fellowship; the Social Science Research Council for an International Dissertation Research Fellowship; the US Bureau of Educational and Cultural Affairs for a Fulbright-Hays Dissertation Research Grant; and the US Department of Education for Foreign Language and Area Studies fellowships (allowing me to study Zulu, Xhosa and Afrikaans for four academic years at Yale and in KwaZulu-Natal).

To the *readers of the first drafts* of this book, wow, I owe you more gratitude than I could ever express. You were generous with your time and insights when I needed them most. Thank you: Mike Callaghan, Ashawnta Jackson, Ashanti Kunene, Susan Levine, Andrew Offenburger, Heidi Sauls, and Dawie Scholtz.

Let me also give a big thank you to Jessica Powers, the dynamic founder and leader of Catalyst Press, who invited me to write this, the inaugural book of the Intimate Geographies series, which I am also proud to further develop as its editor. (Books on Soweto, Lagos, Zurich, and

El Paso coming soon!) This is gonna be fun. Thank you also to Karen Vermeulen for the great map and cover design, and to Kathy McInnis for the excellent text design.

To my *Cape Town family:* Lily-Jade, Nadine, Charmaine, and Tony Botto, the most generous people I know; my *Kaapse Pa*, Edward Jones, who opened up Cape Town's maritime and minstrel world to me; and my *Kaapse Ma*, Charlotte Jones, who has showered me with love and care everyday I've been in Cape Town. I can't imagine life in this city without your warm presence.

To *my parents*, Edgar and Carolyn Trotter, who encouraged my wanderlust and curiosity about the world, thank you for truly everything! You are the best parents a child could ever have. To my brother, Ed, and his family—Tracy, Evan, Neil, Alec, and Luke—it's been fun to share so much of the adventure together. To my brother, John and his daughter, Uriah, I miss you both so much. Thank you as well, dear Laura. And to my grandparents, Henry and Lucy, who played a key role in connecting me to Africa. Thank you all so much.

Lastly, to *my dear wife*, Marjorie, what an amazing time we've had together in Cape Town over the last two decades! And with *our precious daughter*, Sonoya, the adventure continues. Thank you both for your understanding as I've spent so much time writing over the past year. This book I dedicate to you.